T0038114

COELBREN

COELBREN

Traditions, Divination Lore, and Magic of the Welsh Bardic Alphabet

Revised and Expanded Edition

John Michael Greer

AEON

First published in 2017, Llewellyn Worldwide

Second published in 2023 by
Aeon Books

Copyright © 2023 by John Michael Greer

The right of John Michael Greer to be identified as the author of this work has been asserted in accordance with §§ 77 and 78 of the Copyright Design and Patents Act 1988.

All rights reserved. No part of this publication may be reproduced, stored in a retrieval system, or transmitted, in any form or by any means, electronic, mechanical, photocopying, recording, or otherwise, without the prior written permission of the publisher.

British Library Cataloguing in Publication Data

A C.I.P. for this book is available from the British Library

ISBN-13: 978-1-80152-062-1

Typeset by Medlar Publishing Solutions Pvt Ltd, India

www.aeonbooks.co.uk

Einigan the Giant beheld three pillars of light, having in them all demonstrable sciences that ever were, or ever will be. And he took three rods of the quicken tree, and placed on them the forms and signs of all sciences, so as to be remembered; and exhibited them. But those who saw them misunderstood, and falsely apprehended them, and taught illusive sciences, regarding the rods as a God, whereas they only bore His Name. When Einigan saw this he was greatly annoyed, and in the intensity of his grief he broke the three rods, nor were others found that contained accurate sciences. He was so distressed on this account that from the intensity he burst asunder, and with his parting breath he prayed God that there should be accurate sciences among men in the flesh, and there should be a correct understanding for the proper discernment thereof. And at the end of a year and a day after the decease of Einigan, Menw, son of the Three Shouts, beheld three rods growing out of the mouth of Einigan, which exhibited the sciences of the Ten Letters, and the mode in which the sciences of language and speech were arranged by them, and in language and speech all distinguishable sciences. He then took the rods, and taught from them …

—*Barddas*

An earlier and less complete version of this book was previously published in 2017 as *The Coelbren Alphabet: The Lost Oracle of the Welsh Bards*

CONTENTS

ΛΛ<J>ΙΚΓΟΓ

INTRODUCTION

Λ㇄ᐸ⅃ᐳIᛙᒉOᒉ

This book owes its existence to a remarkable and unexpected discovery.

Like many others before me, I had long been interested in the curious, vaguely runic alphabet called the Coelbren of the Bards, which appears in the pages of *Barddas* ("Bardism"), the vast collection of Welsh Druid lore partly compiled and partly invented by Iolo Morganwg in the late eighteenth and early nineteenth centuries.[1] According to the texts included in *Barddas*, the Coelbren had been passed down by a succession of Welsh bards and loremasters since the days of the ancient Druids, and formed the key to a body of hidden lore, *Cyfrinach Beirdd Ynys Prydain*, "the Secret of the Bards of the Isle of Britain."

Practically all scholars today reject the claim that the Coelbren goes back to ancient times, and most believe that Iolo invented the alphabet himself. The Coelbren's roots in the Druid Revival of the eighteenth and nineteenth centuries, though, make the old bardic alphabet a fascinating phenomenon in its own right, and like the other traditions of Druid nature spirituality that emerged from that movement, it needs

---

[1] Recently reprinted as Williams ab Ithel 2004; the discussion of the Coelbren is on pp. 10–97 and 116–166.

no older pedigree. Like so many others over the last three centuries or so, I found my own spiritual home in the heritage of the Druid Revival. I've had the opportunity to contribute more than once to the process of recovering lost or neglected elements of the modern Druid tradition.

The Coelbren was a tempting candidate for a rescue mission of this sort. A great many spiritual traditions around the world have made use of writing systems as an important source of symbolism. The Hebrew alphabet plays an essential role, for example, in the Kabbalah, Judaism's mystical tradition; and *kotodama*—a system of spiritual interpretations of the Japanese *kana* writing systems—has as large a place in Japanese esotericism. The Ogham alphabet of ancient Ireland and Scotland, and the Germanic, Norse, and Anglo-Saxon runes, have a similar function in contemporary Celtic and Germanic paganism.

What gives each of these writing systems the ability to function as potent symbols in divination, meditation, and ritual is that they represent concepts as well as sounds. For example, the Ogham few (letter) Beith, ⊢, represents the birch tree, and also beginnings, purification, and renewal, and the Old English rune Feoh, ᚠ, represents cattle, and also wealth, creativity, and prosperity. The same is true of every other writing system that has been put to use in spiritual, religious, and magical traditions: knowing the meaning as well as the sound of the letters is the key to making the system work.

That was the difficulty with the Coelbren, though. The passages of *Barddas* that discuss the Coelbren have a great deal to say about its origins, history, and traditional uses, but they say nothing about letter meanings or even the names that were used for the individual letters. Lacking those pieces of the puzzle, the Coelbren remained silent. Some attempts had been made to assign meanings and symbolism to the letters in recent years, but those were arbitrary and worked poorly in practice.

In 2013, shortly after the publication of my book *The Celtic Golden Dawn*, I decided to tackle the riddle of the Coelbren, and see if I could find some way to make it work as a symbolic alphabet for modern Druids. Over the months that followed, I read and reread the pages of *Barddas*, and tried to find other resources on the subject, with very limited success. It was clear from certain passages in *Barddas* that the Coelbren letters once had a very important place in Welsh bardic symbolism and teaching. Small wooden sticks with notches were once used, according to one of these passages, to communicate the mysteries of the bards.[2] The Welsh word *coelbren* itself, literally "omen stick," strongly suggested that Coelbren divination was once part of the bardic repertoire—but what the individual letters were named, what they meant, and how they were used for any purpose but writing poems and prose, remained unknown.

By the autumn of 2014 my research was at a standstill. I'd learned everything about the Coelbren that *Barddas* had to offer, and tracked down the few scraps of additional information that earlier researchers had found out about it. I'd also learned about another obscure Welsh alphabet, the Alphabet of Nemnivus, which appears in precisely one old manuscript and may well have been some medieval scribe's idea of a scholarly joke. None of it had brought me any closer to the key to the Coelbren. That's how matters stood when I went with my wife and two friends to visit a big used book store in a neighboring town.

Used book stores in the north central Appalachians aren't the kind of place you expect to find obscure scholarly books on Welsh grammar. Still, tucked in among a random assortment of unrelated books on the foreign-language shelf in the dimmest corner at the back of the shop was a battered hardback reprint of J. Morris Jones's *A Welsh Grammar, Historical and Comparative*, a hefty work of old-fashioned scholarship originally published in 1913. I pulled it off the shelf and opened it to an early page at random, and the first words that caught my eye were "alphabet of Nemnivus." That was intriguing enough, but the rest of the paragraph was even more so: it explained that this alphabet was discussed in a book I've never heard of, by an author whose name I recognized at once: J. Williams ab Ithel.

The Rev. John Williams ab Ithel was a major figure in Welsh Druid circles in the first half of the nineteenth century, and he was also the editor who produced *Barddas* out of a heap of disconnected manuscripts left behind by Iolo Morganwg. The book Morris Jones cited, though, was one I had never encountered: *Dosparth Ederyn Dafod Aur*, a grammar of medieval Welsh that appears to have been compiled or invented by Iolo Morganwg. Edited and translated by Williams ab Ithel, *Dosparth Ederyn Dafod Aur* was published in 1856 and, like most of the products of Iolo Morganwg's circle, dropped out of print and out of sight shortly thereafter. What the alphabet of Nemnivus was doing in such a volume was a puzzle. Had the bardic circles around Iolo Morganwg made use

---

[2] Williams ap Ithel 2004, p. 155.

of that alphabet instead of the Coelbren, I wondered? Or was something else going on?

That night, I set out to find a copy of *Dosparth Ederyn Dafod Aur*. To my delight, it had been scanned and archived on the internet, and within a few minutes my elderly computer was struggling to download a ten and a half megabyte file over a balky connection. A quarter of an hour later, maybe, I started paging through the file. The alphabet of Nemnivus was there; so was the Coelbren of the Bards—and after a few minutes of reading, I found myself staring with my mouth open at the thing that so many people in the Druid community had been pursuing fruitlessly for so many years: a detailed discussion of the symbolic meanings of the Coelbren letters and the inner structure of the alphabet itself, which had been penned by John Williams ab Ithel 160 years before.[3]

To sum up briefly a theme that will be discussed in much more detail in Chapter Two of this book, the secret of the Coelbren isn't a matter of letter names with meanings, like those of the Ogham fews or the runes. Rather, the Coelbren letters take their symbolic meanings directly from the sounds they represent, and from the shapes made by the mouth in the process of pronunciation. As we'll see, there's a long tradition behind this approach, which is called "sound symbolism" by modern linguists.

Once I had that key, it took me only a short time to reconstruct the entire system and begin putting it to the test. The result was everything I hoped it would be—a coherent, effective, and meaningful system of letter symbolism for modern Druids, which can be put to work in divination, meditation, and ritual with excellent results. Other projects delayed the process of putting the system down on paper, but once those were out of the way, my earlier book on the subject, *The Coelbren Alphabet*, took shape promptly. Several years later, I had the opportunity to rewrite that text in the light of further discoveries concerning the Coelbren, including the number values of the letters and several other remarkable findings, and the book in your hands took shape in response to that. As a result, the Coelbren may now take its rightful place as a bardic and Druidical symbolic, divinatory, and magical alphabet.

It might seem surprising that something that was once of central importance to the Welsh Druid movement could have been lost so

---

[3] I have included the relevant passages in this volume as Appendix 3.

completely for so many years. Such things happen all the time in the history of alternative culture, though. Wales has always been richly supplied with poets, but the number of bards who studied with Iolo Morganwg and learned the details of his rituals and symbolism was never large, and a variety of historical forces discussed in Chapter One raised high barriers to the survival of many elements of the bardic tradition that Iolo transmitted and at least partly invented. As far as I have been able to determine, the meanings of the Coelbren letters were published only once, in the pages of Williams ab Ithel's translation of the *Dosparth Ederyn Dafod Aur*, and that was a work so rare and obscure that no one thought to consult it once the living tradition of the Coelbren was interrupted.

The twentieth-century revival of interest in all things Druidical thus missed the old lore completely. By the 1980s, photocopies of *Barddas* were in circulation in various corners of the British and American Druid communities, but no one happened across the clue that sent me to the *Dosparth Ederyn Dafod Aur*, and so the one resource that could have answered the questions *Barddas* raised was never identified. Several writers attempted to come up with meanings for the Coelbren letters, most often borrowing tree-symbolism from the Irish Ogham alphabet for the purpose, while the actual symbolism and meanings of the letters remained lost. Even so careful a scholar as Nigel Pennick, whose *Ogham and Coelbren: Keys to the Celtic Mysteries* was published in 2000, apparently had not encountered *Dosparth Ederyn Dafod Aur* and knew nothing of the sound symbolism of the Coelbren.[4]

The rediscovery of the key to the Coelbren thus opens a fascinating new branch of Druidical study to those who are interested in the old Welsh traditions, and to the broader field of Druidry and Celtic spirituality in general. I have found through practice that the Coelbren makes an effective divinatory oracle, and it's also a rich and flexible symbolic alphabet that can be used for the same spiritual, religious, and magical purposes as other sacred alphabets. All that's needed is the time and patience to master the meanings of the twenty-four Coelbren letters.

This book has been designed and written as a complete introduction to the Coelbren. The first chapter, "The Bard from Glamorgan," introduces Iolo Morganwg and the remarkable revival of Welsh Bardic and Druid traditions he helped set in motion. The second chapter,

---

[4] His survey of the Coelbren is otherwise admirable; see Pennick 2000, pp. 124–134.

"The Coelbren of the Bards," sets out the traditional lore of the Coelbren. The third chapter, "The Letters of the Coelbren," gives the name, keyword, meaning, sound symbolism, and divinatory meaning of each of the twenty-four Coelbren letters, and the fourth chapter, "Coelbren Divination," explains how divination works and presents a series of layouts that can be used to make the Coelbren reveal the hidden patterns of the present and the foreshadowings of the future. The fifth, sixth, and seventh chapters, "Coelbren Symbolism," "Coelbren Meditation," and "Coelbren Magic," extend the Coelbren further into other realms of inner practice. Finally, two appendices sum up the divinatory possibilities of the Coelbren and discuss how the old oracle of the bards can be used in conjunction with the system of Druid spirituality and magic I've presented and discussed in my book *The Celtic Golden Dawn*, while a third appendix gives the original text of Williams ab Ithel's discussion of the Coelbren.

A few acknowledgments are due at this point. Two of the people who contributed the most to this project have since passed into the Otherworld of which Celtic authors wrote so vividly: Corby Ingold, who introduced me to modern Druidry and officiated at my initiation into the Order of Bards Ovates and Druids, and John Gilbert, who initiated me into the Ancient Order of Druids in America and passed on to me a body of occult lore that still guides my practices today. I am also indebted to Philip Carr-Gomm, past Chosen Chief of the Order of Bards Ovates and Druids, for access to the archives of that order and thus to a great deal of valuable Druid lore that has helped guide this project in many ways. On another level, the members of the Druidical Order of the Golden Dawn deserve thanks for their interest in the Coelbren and their enthusiastic exploration of its possibilities. Finally, I owe a debt to Oliver Rathbone of Aeon Books for making this second and much-improved edition possible. My thanks go with all.

CHAPTER ONE

The bard from Glamorgan

ΛレＣ⅃＞ＩﾄﾄＯﾄ

> The three necessary functions of a Bard: to teach and explain all things in the face of the sun and the eye of light; to praise all that is excellent and good; and to substitute peace for devastation and pillage.
>
> —*Barddas*[5]

The leaves were turning their fall colors on Primrose Hill, on the northern side of Regents Park in London, as a line of people filed out of a pub and walked together through the streets toward the hilltop. Most of them were young, and all of them wore the colorful garments that were fashionable just then; some had ribbons, blue, green, or white, tied around their right arms above the elbow. Passersby looked on in bemusement as the group reached the hilltop and formed a circle. The leader of the group, a forty-something man in a bright blue coat whose unruly brown hair fluttered around his face in the breeze, went to the center of the circle and called out: "Is there peace?" The people in the circle responded together, "Peace." The celebration of the autumn

---

[5] Williams ab Ithel 2004, vol. 2., p. 57.

equinox, following traditions that the group's leader claimed to trace back to the time of the ancient Druids, had formally begun.

Many people who are alive today remember nearly identical happenings in the London counterculture scene of the 1960s and 1970s, in the first years of today's revival of interest in all things Celtic. Yellowing newspaper clippings in old archives tell of similar events back in the 1920s, when an earlier wave of enthusiasm for Celtic traditions was in full spate. The events I have just described, though, don't belong to either of those eras. They took place on September 23, 1792. On that day George III was on the English throne, and English men and women were already beginning to dress in the styles that would make the Regency era one of the great ages of gorgeous attire. Across the Channel, revolutionary violence gripped France, and the cannonade of Valmy just three days before the equinox ceremony marked the beginning of an era of European wars that would not end until the carnage of Waterloo nearly twenty-three years later. On the far side of the Atlantic, George Washington was nearing the end of his first term as president of the newly founded United States. This was the world into which Iolo Morganwg, a poet and stonecutter from the county of Glamorgan in Wales, launched what he claimed were the teachings of the ancient Welsh bards.

Wales and England

To understand Iolo and his impact, it's necessary to start with Wales, the mountainous principality on the western flank of the island of Britain. Some twelve centuries before Iolo's time, as the Roman Empire tumbled into ruin, what was then the province of Britannia was ravaged by armed invasions from the barbarian countries of northern Europe. The Angles, Saxons, and Jutes—three closely related tribal peoples who lived in what is now northern Germany and Denmark—took advantage of the collapse of Roman rule and their own mastery of the seas to swarm across to Britain's poorly defended shores. Over the centuries that followed, the bulk of the island fell into their hands, becoming Angle-land, or as we now say it, England. Their languages blended together to become the ancestor of modern English, and their customs and culture laid the foundation on which their descendants and later waves of invaders built what is now the English nation.

The mountainous regions in the north and west of the island remained independent when the lowlands fell, however, and their history unfolded along a different path. In the immediate wake of the English conquests, four independent Celtic nations held parts of Britain: from north to south, Scotland, Rheged, Wales, and Cornwall. Rheged was overwhelmed by the Northumbrian Saxons in the seventh century, and only scraps of its ancient Celtic culture and language survive. Cornwall was conquered by the Saxon kingdom of Wessex in the ninth century but remained a nation apart, and the old Cornish language has been revived and is spoken there today. Scotland had a more complex history, for most of its traditional Celtic culture arrived in post-Roman times with immigrants from Ireland, and its Celtic language, Scots Gaelic, is closely related to Irish. Its earlier Celtic peoples, the Picts, spoke a language related to Cornish and Welsh, but they faded out of history during the turmoil of the Dark Ages.

Then there was Wales: "Wild Wales," as the prophecies of the Welsh bard Taliesin called it, a land of rugged mountains and steep-sided valleys between the rolling hills of the English Midlands and the cold waters of the Irish Sea. It was invaded repeatedly by English armies and finally conquered by King Edward I of England in 1282, but it retained its own distinctive laws and legal system until the sixteenth century. To this day the language, culture, and customs of the Welsh remain sharply different from those of their English neighbors to the east.

Among the jewels of Welsh culture is the oldest living tradition of poetry in Europe, a heritage that can be traced back in an unbroken lineage to the sixth century. The bard—this English term is actually a borrowing from the Welsh word *bardd*—has always been an important figure in Welsh communities, a learned and respected person filling roles in society that few other cultures assign to poets. A properly trained bard was expected not only to be able to compose verses in the demanding meters of traditional Welsh poetry, but also to have by heart a wealth of traditional tales, to preserve local genealogies and histories, and to serve as a general source of learning and lore for the community in which he lived.

These duties, however, became steadily harder to fulfill as England entered the Industrial Revolution, and wealth and power became ever more concentrated in the hands of the bankers and merchants of London and the industrialists of the English Midlands. By the middle years of the eighteenth century, the Welsh poetic traditions were carried on mostly by part-time bards who supported themselves with day jobs, while too many other Welsh people had little time for poetry in an age when brutal poverty was the norm. The cultures of all the Celtic nations were widely condemned and despised as relics of a barbarous past. Those who clung to Welsh culture in the teeth of English public opinion faced a rising tide of social and legal penalties. It was in this setting that Iolo Morganwg was born.

A bardic apprenticeship

His real name was Edward Williams, and he was born in 1747 in the little village of Pennon in the county of Glamorgan in Wales. His father was a stonemason and young Edward took up the same trade, traveling to various corners of Wales and England in search of work. In his teen years, however, he met some of the few remaining Welsh bards—Lewis Hopkin, Rhys Morgan, and especially Siôn Bradford, who became his most important instructor. From them he learned the rules of bardic verse and gained an enduring love of the Welsh language and its poetry. His travels in Wales gave him the opportunity to visit libraries and manuscript collections around the principality, and sparked a taste for copying and collecting old Welsh manuscripts that lasted for the rest of his life. It was customary for the bards of his day to adopt a pen name in Welsh. Edward Williams followed suit, adopting the name by which he would be remembered ever after—Iolo Morganwg, "Ned of Glamorgan."

In 1773 he moved to London and quickly made contacts in the Welsh expatriate scene there, becoming a member of the recently founded Gwyneddigion Society, an organization devoted to Welsh historical scholarship. Combined with his training in traditional bardic verse and his enthusiasm for old manuscripts, the historical background and access to documents he gained by way of London's Welsh community gave him a thorough grounding in the ancient literature of the principality, and he turned out to have a remarkable talent for the language and poetry of medieval Wales.

It was also during this first period in London that he first encountered the writings of the fourteenth-century bard Dafydd ap Gwilym, one of the greatest of Welsh poets. Iolo was bowled over by the power of Dafydd's verse and the effortless way in which the old bard handled even the most demanding of formal Welsh poetic forms. Reading and rereading Dafydd's poems, Iolo felt transported back to an older and better time, when bards could still count on financial support from aristocrats such as Dafydd's patron Ifor Hael, and the scars of the new industrial system had not yet begun to deface the Welsh landscape with coal mines and smokestacks.

Daydreams do not pay the bills, though, and London had plenty of stonemasons. He traveled to Kent and worked there for a time, but business was not much better. In 1777 he returned home to Glamorgan and married, determined to settle down, open a business of some kind, and earn the kind of steady income that would allow him to pursue his poetic and scholarly interests with some degree of comfort and financial security.

Unfortunately for his plans, Iolo had no talent for business at all. Each of the schemes he launched to try to better his situation collapsed around him, leaving him so far in debt that he spent a while in debtor's prison. When his wife Margaret inherited a farm from her parents, he gave farming a try, and had only slightly better luck. It didn't help that in his London days, Iolo had picked up the habit of using laudanum—opium dissolved in alcohol, which was legal and readily available in Britain at that time—and his drug habit gave him no help at all in dealing with the hard realities of business or farming.

Still, the main problem Iolo faced was that he was brilliantly qualified for a profession that no longer existed—court bard to a medieval Welsh aristocrat—and not really suited to anything else. He knew the old bardic teachings inside and out, he had the traditions and lore of his native county at his fingertips, and he could, at the drop of a hat, craft first-rate verse in medieval Welsh using any of the classic poetic forms. The sole downside was that nobody in eighteenth-century Britain was willing to pay for medieval Welsh poetry written by a modern poet named Edward Williams.

But if those same poems had Dafydd ap Gwilym's name on them ...

The forger

It was a propitious time for such ventures, for the late eighteenth century was one of the great ages of literary forgery. When Iolo was fourteen years old, in 1761, a Scottish poet and collector of traditional tales named James MacPherson claimed to have discovered an epic poem in the Scots Gaelic language, titled *Fingal*, which had been written by the ancient bard Ossian.[6] His English version of the poem was an immediate bestseller, and was followed two years later by another epic poem by the same bard titled *Temora*. The Ossian poems, as they came to be called, found enthusiastic readers across Europe—Napoleon, to mention only one famous name, was a passionate fan, and carried a volume of MacPherson's poems on all his military campaigns. MacPherson refused to show scholars the Gaelic originals or explain a range of details that didn't fit, though, and it came out eventually that he had simply gathered up an assortment of traditional Highland tales about the hero Fionn and his son Oisín, strung them together into a single narrative, and written the poems himself.

Around the time that hard questions were first being asked about the Ossian poems, in turn, a teenager from Bristol named Thomas Chatterton astonished and delighted the English literary world by discovering the manuscripts of a previously unknown medieval poet of the fifteenth century, Thomas Rowley. After Chatterton committed suicide in 1770 at the age of seventeen, it turned out that he had written all of the Rowley manuscripts himself.

MacPherson and Chatterton were only two of the brightest stars in the glittering sky of eighteenth-century forgery, and the thought of imitating the success of MacPherson's work, in particular, must have been tempting to Iolo. He was familiar with the controversies surrounding both men, and seems to have paid close attention to their mistakes.[7] Unlike MacPherson, he had no need to worry if he were asked to show verses in the original language, and his grasp of medieval Welsh was much more complete than Chatterton's knowledge of medieval English. For a man living on the brink of destitution with a wife and children to support, he was also surprisingly patient. He moved into the business of forgery slowly, without the sudden rush of discoveries that roused suspicions about MacPherson and Chatterton.

It was thus early in the 1780s that he first mentioned, in letters to scholarly Welsh friends in London, that there were poems by Dafydd ap Gwilym in Glamorgan that didn't seem to be in the manuscript collections elsewhere. Two of those friends, Owen Jones and William Owen Pughe, just happened to be assembling the first published collection

---

[6] This name is more properly spelled Oisín, and pronounced "Usheen."
[7] Constantine 2007 is an excellent introduction to the issues surrounding Iolo's forgeries.

of Dafydd's poems just then, and eagerly wrote back for more details. In due course, when *Barddoniaeth Dafydd ab Gwilym* (*The Poetry of Dafydd ap Gwilym*) saw print in 1789, it included a number of Iolo's forged poems. These were promptly hailed as among Dafydd's best work.

More forgeries followed in due course. Meanwhile, with an eye toward achieving a more conventional sort of literary success, Iolo got to work on a collection of verse in English, to be titled *Poems Lyric and Pastoral*. Crowdsourcing may be the latest thing in today's internet culture, but it was already a familiar process in Iolo's time; poets or writers who didn't have the funds to pay for the printing of their works could put advertisements in literary periodicals, soliciting subscribers to pay for copies in advance. That was how *Poems Lyric and Pastoral* was published. Among the many people who contributed was a plantation owner and military officer in the former British colony of Virginia, who had become famous by the time the book finally saw print in 1794. His name was George Washington.[8]

The gorsedd of the bards

In 1791, with high hopes of launching a writing career, Iolo returned to London, but his lifelong bad luck at business continued to pursue him. *Poems Lyrical and Pastoral* went through one delay after another on its way to publication, and other opportunities were few and far between. A large part of his writing time, furthermore, went into projects that would not help pay his bills—above all, into the first drafts of a series of documents outlining the history, teachings, and customs of the ancient Welsh bards.

A mystery that will probably never be solved surrounds these documents, which were finally published long after Iolo's death in a collection titled *Barddas* (*Bardism*). By the time Iolo returned to London, he was an accomplished forger of medieval Welsh poems and literature. Equally, by the time Iolo returned to London, he had traveled through much of Wales and copied a great many old documents, many of which were later lost or destroyed. Even those scholars who criticize Iolo's forgeries in the harshest terms have been forced to admit, for example, that his collection of southern Welsh folk music—*Ancient National Airs of Gwent and Morganwg* (published posthumously in 1844)—is full of

---

[8] Williams 1794, p. xxxviii.

authentic traditional songs and tunes, and that some of the other documents he unearthed were in fact authentic discoveries rather than forgeries.

The old manuscripts of Wales in those days were scattered far and wide. Local gentry and clergy all over the Welsh countryside had their own collections, and it was far from rare for ordinary farm families to have inherited a manuscript volume or two, which might contain copies of poetry and tales found nowhere else. Wales at that time was a literary collector's paradise, since any random farmhouse might hide some lost literary treasure. It was also a forger's paradise for the same reason. Most of what survived of the literary heritage of old Wales consisted of copies of copies, as often as not riddled with mistakes. If Iolo said that he'd found a poem supposedly by Dafydd Gwilym in a volume kept by a farmer in a remote corner of Glamorgan, few people were able or willing to tackle the long journey that was needed in those days to see if he was telling the truth. What's more, if some of the fine details of the poem's grammar and verse structure weren't quite right for the fourteenth century, who was to say that those errors hadn't been accidentally inserted by some clumsy copyist?

The mystery surrounding Iolo's bardic documents is thus simply that nobody knows which parts of his bardic lore came from one of the many documents that Iolo is known to have studied, but have been lost since his time, and which parts came from his own vivid imagination. There are things in *Barddas* that are almost certainly Iolo's inventions, but there are also things in the collection that are very hard to explain unless Iolo did in fact draw on sources that dated from the Middle Ages.[9] In some cases—for example, the *Meddygon Myddfai* (*Physicians of Myddfai*), a collection of recipes for herbal medicines—it's been shown by scholars that Iolo found an actual Welsh document and then rewrote it, adding additional material.[10] The possibility that some of the papers collected in *Barddas* could have come out of some similar process can't be dismissed out of hand.

It was his work on the traditions and institutions of the ancient bards that gave rise to the ceremony described at the start of this chapter. According to Iolo, a gorsedd of bards—the word *gorsedd* in Welsh means "throne," and refers to the chair of the presiding bard; the plural

---

[9] See, for example, Greer 2004.
[10] Constantine 2007, p. 24.

is *gorseddau*—was the traditional assembly of bards, held on the solstices and equinoxes. At these events, candidates for bardic training were formally accepted, those who had completed their training received the honored title of *Bardd Braint a Defod* (Bard by Right and Privilege), and decisions relating to the bardic institution and its traditions were debated and handed down. A gorsedd had to be held out of doors— "in the face of the sun, the eye of light"—which explains the scene that startled passersby near Primrose Hill on that autumn day.

Iolo held at least three gorseddau in London; he may have held others, but those are the ones from which records survive. By the time he left London again in 1795, his failed dreams of literary success had been replaced by a stranger and more potent vision—the dream of resurrecting the bardic institutions of Wales in all the glory that he had imagined for them.

The secret of the bards of the island of Britain

Iolo spent the last thirty years of his life in this eccentric quest. Amazingly, the success that had eluded him in every other pursuit finally came to him. Supported mostly by the generosity of his many friends and admirers, he alternated periods of writing and teaching at home with long journeys throughout Glamorgan and other parts of Wales, handing on the traditions and customs of Welsh bardism to anyone who wanted to learn them. He founded gorseddau wherever there were poets qualified to lead them—at one point in his life, for example, the small town of Merthyr Tydfil boasted no fewer than three independent gorseddau. In the process he attracted a circle of disciples as passionate about his bardic teachings as he was. His son Taliesin was among these. Another, the most influential in the long run, was a young Anglican priest from Merioneth named John Williams, who in later years—as John Williams ab Ithel—would play a crucial role in transmitting his teacher's legacy to the future.

To his bardic students, Iolo handed on an extraordinary body of lore, symbolism, and wisdom teaching. According to him, bardism dated back to the beginning of the world, when Einigan the Giant, the Welsh Adam, witnessed the three descending rays of light that brought the world into being. In those rays of light was all the knowledge that ever was or would be, and Einigan, beholding them, understood some of that knowledge. In order to preserve what he had learned, he took three long straight branches of a rowan tree, cut them into staves, and carved the first of all letters on them. Some time afterward, though, others who encountered the three staves worshipped them as gods instead of learning the wisdom that was written on them, and Einigan was so distressed by this that his heart burst and he died.[11]

A year and a day after Einigan's death, the story continues, Menw the Old happened upon the giant's skull, lying neglected in a field. Through the skull's eye sockets and mouth grew the three rowan staves, which had taken root and sprouted leaves—and the wisdom that had been carved upon the staves was still partly legible. Studying that wisdom, Menw became the first of the Gwyddoniaid, the loremasters of the Welsh people in the distant past, before Hu the Mighty led them to the shores of Britain. It was after the Welsh came to Britain that the Gwyddoniaid were divided into the three orders of ovates, bards, and druids, and the bards received their portion of the wisdom of Einigan to transmit down the centuries.

It must have been an astonishing experience to sit with Iolo around the table in his home, or in some clergyman's house or rural inn where he stayed for a few days while traveling, and listen to the old bard as he conjured up the luminous images of a Welsh past that never was. By this time, between his laudanum habit and his own passionate commitment to his vision, Iolo himself had long since lost track of his own role in inventing the bardic mysteries he taught. With shining eyes and sweeping gestures, he spoke of the cycles of reincarnation by which souls worked their way up from the simplest living things through all the forms of the animal creation to humanity and then beyond, into the realm of Gwynfydd, the Luminous Life;[12] he expounded the customs and traditions of the bardic assemblies; he taught his pupils how to write in the ancient Bardic alphabet, the Coelbren of the Bards, and hinted at the existence of a secret hidden away in the Coelbren that was known only to properly initiated bards.

Cyfrinach Beirdd Ynys Prydain, the Secret of the Bards of the Isle of Britain, was the heart of Iolo's teaching. What it was has never been publicly revealed. It was communicated to a properly prepared bardic student by his teacher, under a vow of secrecy, and it could not be revealed to anyone other than a bard without forfeiting all the rights

---

[11] Williams ab Ithel 2004, pp. 48–51.
[12] Williams ab Ithel 2004, pp. 226–235.

and privileges of bardic status. According to *Barddas*, it had to do with the true name of God, which was somehow concealed in the emblem of the three rays of light, /|\.

In his introduction to *Dosparth Ederyn Davod Aur*, John Williams ab Ithel passed on certain cryptic hints about the nature of the great bardic secret:

> This form /|\ was the A wen (awen) the blessed A, said to contain all the other letters, because they are but modifications of it; and all sciences, not only because they are represented by letters, but because they can be learned from an acquaintance with the several attributes of God, which are exhibited in the symbol of His Name. An instance of the development of the primary character, and of the formation of additional letters, may be found in | /|\ \|/ or IAU, one of the forms in which the Divine Name is written.[13]

Cryptic as it is, this passage points in unexpected directions. The Welsh word *awen* means "inspiration"; it appears frequently in bardic poetry to indicate the spirit of inspiration that descended on the inspired poet. In the Middle Ages, according to the chronicler Gerald of Wales, people known as *awenyddion*—"those with awen"—were found throughout Wales; they could foretell the future by going into trance and being possessed by awen.[14] Williams ab Ithel read the word awen as A *wen*, "blessed A" in Welsh—"pure a" is another possible translation—and treated the emblem of the three rays of light as the letter A, while the

same letter upside down was U or W. These preceded by the single vertical line meaning I spelled one of the names of God, IAU or, as it was usually spelled, IAO. This is the great name of God in Gnostic tradition. Why it appears in Williams ab Ithel's book and also in *Barddas* is a fascinating question; to answer it may be to reveal the secret that Iolo concealed in his rituals and symbols.

The same secret could also be found in the Dasgubell Rodd—a phrase that means "gift besom"[15] in Welsh—but

---

[13] Williams ab Ithel 1856, p. x.

[14] Gerald of Wales 1978, p. 246.

[15] A besom is an old-fashioned broom made of twigs tied around the bottom of a long handle.

neither *Barddas* nor any other collection of Iolo's writings reveals what the Dasgubell Rodd is. It may not be accidental, however, that if you take the letters Williams ab Ithel gave for IAU and write them in a different order, as shown on the left, the result does look like an old-fashioned besom. Here is what Iolo had to say about the Dasgubell Rodd, in dialogue form:

Q. What is the Dasgubell Rodd?
A. The key to the primitive Coelbren.
Q. What is it that explains the primitive Coelbren?
A. The Dasgubell Rodd.
Q. What else?
A. The secret of the Dasgubell Rodd.
Q. What secret?
A. The secret of the Bards of the Isle of Britain.
Q. What will divulge the secret of the Bards of the Isle of Britain?
A. Instruction by a master in virtue of a vow.
Q. What kind of vow?
A. A vow made with God.[16]

The legacy of Iolo Morganwg

The sheer scale of Iolo's achievement in his final years is among the most remarkable things about his far from ordinary life. Serene in the conviction that he spoke for the bardic traditions of antiquity, he called on the poets of nineteenth-century Wales to embrace the customs and institutions that he had invented. Astonishingly, that's exactly what they did. The turning point in that process came in 1819, when an eisteddfod (bardic competition) held in Carmarthen invited him to conduct a gorsedd of bards as part of the ceremonies. That established a tradition that was honored by subsequent eisteddfodau across Wales, and is still honored to this day: go to the Welsh National Eisteddfod, which is held annually in Wales, and you'll see Iolo's rituals enacted in gorgeous costumes and antique pomp.

The popularity of the bardic gorsedd had a significant impact on Welsh cultural history in the nineteenth century. Under its patronage, the rebirth of Welsh scholarship that had been launched by expatriates

---

[16] Williams ab Ithel 2004, pp. 165–167.

in London late in the previous century spread explosively through Wales. Once the long ordeal of the Napoleonic Wars ended, local societies for Welsh learning and culture sprang up across the principality, and hosting an eisteddfod and gorsedd was a popular way for those societies to proclaim their enthusiasm for Welsh tradition. In the wake of this revival, a growing number of Welsh men and women began to take pride once again in their language and culture. Many other people contributed to that transformation, of course, but historians today consider Iolo Morganwg to have been a crucial figure in forging—in both senses of the word—the modern Welsh nation.

His impact was helped along considerably after his death by John Williams ab Ithel, the disciple of Iolo's mentioned above. A capable scholar with a solid command of the medieval Welsh language, Williams ab Ithel was a working clergyman but devoted his off hours to a series of important editions and translations of old Welsh literature. One of those was the *Dosparth Ederyn Dafod Aur*, the medieval treatise on Welsh grammar mentioned in the introduction to this book. His last and greatest project was the creation of *Barddas*, the handbook of bardic lore Iolo had envisioned but never managed to produce. Assembling the fragmentary manuscripts Iolo left behind was an immense chore, but for Williams ab Ithel it was a labor of love. The hefty volume saw print shortly before his death in 1862, and found plenty of readers—and not only in Wales.

Over the course of the nineteenth century, the revival of Celtic culture that Iolo helped set in motion spread far beyond his native principality. South across the Channel from Cornwall and Wales is Brittany, one of the two surviving Celtic nations on the European continent— the other is Galicia in the northwest corner of the Iberian peninsula. Brittany's relationship with France closely parallels the Welsh experience with England, and so it was not surprising that Bretons would be inspired by the example of their relatives to the north. In 1899 a group of Breton poets and scholars were formally made members of the Welsh Gorsedd at a ceremony at Cardiff in Wales, and the next year the Goursez Vreizh (Breton Gorsedd) held its first formal meeting in the Breton town of Guingamp. Cornwall followed suit in 1928, when a delegation of Cornish poets and scholars were inducted at the Welsh Gorsedd in Treorchy, and then held the first celebration of the Gorsedh Kernow (Cornish Gorsedd) at the stone circle at Boscawen-Un. Both these are still active. Less successful in the long run was a Gorsedd of the United States organized among Welsh expatriates in America, which flourished between the two world wars but went out of existence thereafter.

The remarkable popularity of the gorsedd movement had many positive results, but it also had its inevitable downsides. As the movement focused ever more tightly on the preservation of the language, literature, and culture of the three Celtic nations that adopted it,[17] the stranger and more visionary aspects of Iolo's bardic lore got pushed to the sidelines. Iolo's Bardism was neither the first nor the last tradition to lose track of much of its uniqueness in the process of becoming popular—that's a common event in the history of alternative culture. Its importance in the story told here is simply that this is how the Coelbren of the Bards dropped out of common use, and the meanings of the Coelbren letters were forgotten.

There were dissident groups outside the mainstream of the Welsh Gorsedd that kept up the wilder aspects of Iolo's heritage. The most important of them was an independent gorsedd in Pontyprydd, in Iolo's own home county of Glamorgan. Two eccentric and charismatic archdruids—Evan Davies, whose bardic name was Myfyr Morganwg, and his successor Owen Morgan, better known in his time as the irrepressible Archdruid Morien—kept Iolo's bardic mysteries in circulation into the 1920s, and for a time had students across Wales and in America as well.[18] Many aspects of Iolo's teachings have gone on to become important in traditions of spirituality around the world that draw inspiration from the legacy of the Celtic peoples.[19]

The Coelbren of the Bards followed a similar trajectory. In Iolo's last years, and for some decades after his death, a great many Welsh poets took the time to learn how to write in it, and a fair number of Welsh museums still have poems written in the Coelbren on wooden sticks as part of their collections. Later on, as Iolo's forgeries came to light, the Welsh Gorsedd quietly distanced itself from him, and the Coelbren was one of many things that were dropped in that process. It's possible that teachings about the Coelbren are still passed on to those who

---

[17] Important cultural and linguistic differences, as well as ancient rivalries, separate these three Celtic nations from Ireland, Scotland, and the Isle of Man, and thus no effort seems to have been made to export the gorsedd movement to any of these nations.

[18] Bonwick 1983, p. 3.

[19] Greer 2006 is one example out of many.

are admitted to the rank of *Bardd Braint a Defod* by the three surviving gorsedds, and they may even be instructed in the Secret of the Bards of the Isle of Britain, but that will only be known by those who have undergone the ceremony in question.

Some knowledge of the Coelbren seems to have lingered in the occult community long after it vanished elsewhere. Among the artifacts displayed in the recent exhibition of William Butler Yeats's magical equipment at the National Library of Ireland was a painted wooden disk the size of a magical pentacle. In the center was the word Eire in Coelbren, and in the four quarters, also in Coelbren, were the names of the four castles of the Tuatha de Danaan, the wizard-folk of Irish legend: Gorias, Falias, Finias, and Murias. Unsurprisingly, the curators of the exhibit didn't recognize the writing, and described it as "runic."

As far as I have been able to tell, however, the magical community forgot about the Coelbren after the Second World War. All that remained of the Coelbren thereafter were teachings buried in a handful of old books—but as we'll see, there are good reasons to change that, and bring the Coelbren of the Bards back into the widespread use Iolo envisioned for it.

CHAPTER TWO

The Coelbren of the bards

ᚪᛚᚳᛄᛋᛁᚳᚱᚩᚱ

In the early times of the nation of the Cymry letters were called cuttings; and it was after the time of Beli, son of Manogan, that they were called letters. Previously, there were no letters but the primary cuttings, which had been a secret from the age of ages among the Bards of the Isle of Britain, for the preservation of the memorials of country and nation. Beli the Great made them into sixteen, and divulged that arrangement, and appointed that there should never again be a concealment of the sciences of letters, in respect of the arrangement which he made; but he left the ten cuttings a secret.

—*Barddas*[20]

So what is the Coelbren of the Bards, the mysterious writing that concealed the Secret of the Bards of the Isle of Britain? In its most common form—the one used in this book—it's an alphabet of twenty-four letters that are designed to be cut or scratched on wood or stone. Each letter stands for one of the sounds of the Welsh language, and each letter

---

[20] Williams ab Ithel 2004, p. 59.

also has an additional meaning, deriving from its sound, that makes it useful in divination, magic, and certain other forms of spiritual practice.

It's surprisingly common these days for historians of Welsh culture to dismiss the Coelbren, as though it wasn't actually an alphabet at all. The website of the National Museum of Wales, for example, labels it a "false alphabet."[21] That's a very odd thing to say in this context, because the Coelbren is nothing of the kind.

If the phrase "false alphabet" means anything, after all, it means something that looks like an alphabet but doesn't actually spell out words. Such things exist, but the Coelbren isn't one of them. The Coelbren is an actual alphabet: that is, a set of signs that can be used to write out words in a language as a series of individual sounds—phonemes, in the jargon of linguistics. What's more, Welsh bards in the nineteenth century routinely wrote poems in the Coelbren, so it's not just an alphabet that *can* be used, it's an alphabet that *has* been used.

The reason so many scholars dismiss the Coelbren in this way is simply that they believe that Iolo Morganwg invented it. They may well be right, as we've seen, but that doesn't make the Coelbren a "false alphabet"—it just means that it's one of the many writing systems that were invented by a specific person known to history. Back in the ninth century, for example, the Japanese Buddhist monk Kobo Daishi invented the *hiragana* and *katakana* writing systems that people in Japan use to this day. In the middle years of the nineteenth century, similarly, the Native American scholar and activist Sequoyah invented a writing system for Cherokee—but nobody calls these "false writing systems."

In much the same way, more than two centuries ago, Iolo Morganwg gave Wales and the world a set of symbols, ceremonies, and traditions that went on to play a crucial role in reviving the cultural and spiritual heritage of the Welsh people. His work still serves that same role today—in Wales, Cornwall, and Brittany, as part of the Gorsedd movement that continues to preserve the traditions of Celtic culture in those countries, and all over the world, where Iolo's ideas have been put to work in a variety of creative ways for those who feel called to the spiritual heritage of the Celts. The reality of that accomplishment is far more important than whatever history Iolo's bardic lore may or may not have had before his time.

---

[21] See National Museum of Wales 2014.

In a study of another set of controversial claims about a spiritual tradition, Richard W. DeMille has drawn a useful distinction between *authenticity* and *validity*.[22] Authenticity, he points out, relates to whether a given tradition actually comes from the sources claimed for it, while validity relates to whether a given tradition does what it's supposed to do. These two things are often confused, but they don't actually have much to do with one another. Consider the poems that Iolo Morganwg wrote and passed off as Dafydd ap Gwilym's work. They're not authentic—that is, Dafydd ap Gwilym didn't write them—but they are valid—that is, they're first-rate poems that follow all the rules of traditional Welsh verse, and bring just as much delight to the reader as they would do if they were actually by Dafydd ap Gwilym.[23]

It's in this spirit that we can approach the Coelbren, as one of the many creative legacies of the Celtic revival of the late eighteenth and early nineteenth centuries, probably inauthentic but, in its proper context, entirely valid. Iolo himself considered the Coelbren to be a core element of the Bardic teachings that he passed on to his students and the world. As we'll see, there's good reason for that assessment, for the Coelbren letters are not simply a dead alphabet from the past. They have a fascinating range of potential applications here and now.

The legendary history of the Coelbren

One of the things that make the Coelbren distinctive is also one of the things that irritates historians the most about it: the way that Iolo equipped his bardic alphabet with a legendary history dating back to ancient times. Very few invented writing systems have anything of the kind. Even when some invented writing system is said to date back many centuries, nearly always there's just a single version, which supposedly remained unchanged through time while everything else changed around it.[24] The Coelbren, on the other hand, is said to have changed and adapted in much the same way that real scripts do, and

---

[22] DeMille 1980.

[23] See Constantine 2007, pp. 31–37, for a sensitive translation and analysis of one of these, "I Yrru yn Haf i Annerch Morgannwg" ("Sending the Summer to Greet Glamorgan").

[24] The one exception known to me is the openly fictional Elvish writing of J. R. R. Tolkien's Middle-earth; Tolkien was too good a philologist to miss the chance to give his Tengwar and Cirth alphabets histories of their own.

the version of the alphabet that Iolo taught in the nineteenth century was said by him to be only the latest of many forms.

While the legendary history of the Coelbren is rare for an invented script, it follows a pattern common to many contemporary spiritual traditions. Avery Morrow, in a fascinating discussion of Japanese *Kamiyo moji* ("writing of the gods")—a set of scripts that have remarkable parallels with the Coelbren—calls these alternative narratives of the past *parahistories*.[25] As he points out, all histories, even those that are officially accepted, are as much about the present as the past; we turn to history to tell us who we are and how we got here, and alternative visions of the past can thus be powerful tools for re-envisioning ourselves and the world. Iolo's achievements offer solid evidence that Morrow is quite correct. The vision of Welsh history Iolo put into circulation, with the Coelbren at its heart, had a potent influence on the reawakening of Welsh national pride and purpose in the nineteenth century, and continues to exert an influence far beyond the borders of Wales to this day.

That vision goes back a good deal further than modern history does. According to Iolo, as already noted, bardism dates back to the origin of the world, and the Coelbren is just as old. When Einigan the Giant witnessed the three rays of light that created the world, and carved the wisdom he learned from the rays on three rowan staves, those staves became the first written document in the history of the Coelbren. His choice of a writing medium, in turn, set a pattern that would be followed throughout the history of the Coelbren of the Bards.

The Coelbren is in fact primarily designed to be scratched or cut onto wooden sticks, rather than written on paper. Its letters are composed entirely from the vertical and diagonal lines that represent the original three rays of light, /|\. This has symbolic importance, but it's also highly practical for an alphabet meant to be carved into wood: curves are difficult to make quickly and cleanly with a knife, and horizontal lines tend to make the wood split along the length of the stick, obscuring other letters. The Coelbren letters thus have no curves and no horizontal lines—that's something they have in common with other alphabets, such as Ogham and runes, which were also meant to be cut or scratched on wood and other hard surfaces.

---

[25] Morrow 2014, pp. 1–30.

The three rays of light were the first Coelbren, but the first practical form of the alphabet consisted of ten letters, ABCEDILROS or APCE-TILROS; conveniently enough, this was also this alphabet's name. So small a number of letters might seem inadequate for a writing system, and in many other languages it would be. Welsh, however, shares with its sister languages of the Celtic family a great deal of fluidity in conso-nant sounds.

In Welsh, the sounds represented by the letters P, B, Ff (equivalent to English F), F (equivalent to V), and M are, if not quite interchangeable, then closely related and liable to flow into one another. Depending on its place and grammatical function in a sentence, for example, the name of the god Bran can be pronounced Vran or Mran, and the name of the hero Pryderi can turn into Bryderi, Mhryderi, and Phryderi. The same flexibility connects T, D, Th, Dd, and N—in Welsh, Dd is pronounced like the "th" in "these clothes"—and C, G, Ch, Gh, and Ng. In the origi-nal ten-letter Coelbren, one letter did duty for each of these three clus-ters of related sounds.

According to the Bardic legends handed down by Iolo, and quite possibly made up by him as well, the ten-letter Coelbren or Abcedilros was invented by Menw the Old, who discovered the three rowan staves after Einigan's death. Later loremasters added M and N as independent letters, and the resulting alphabet was called Mabcednilros. These two alphabets were kept secret among the ancient Gwyddoniaid, the lore-masters of the Welsh people in the most ancient times, because anyone who knew them could decipher the Secret of the Bards of the Isle of Britain. Later, on, when the Gwyddoniaid were divided into the three orders of druids, bards, and ovates, the bards kept the ten letters of the Abcedilros as one of their secrets. As noted in the previous chapter, it's entirely possible that the Welsh National Gorsedd, the inheritor of Iolo's bardic traditions, still preserves the secret, but only the initiates of that proud and deeply conservative body will ever know the truth of the matter.

The history of the Coelbren does not end with the Abcedilros, though, or even with the Mabcednilros. According to several of the documents that were included in *Barddas*, either Dyfnwal Moelmud or his son Beli the Great—two legendary figures from Britain's pre-Roman past—later established a new Coelbren of sixteen letters. This was not a secret limited to bards; it was an alphabet meant for every literate person, according to *Barddas*, and so came into general use throughout Britain.

There are several versions of the Coelbren of sixteen letters given in the documents in *Barddas*. The most common list runs as follows.

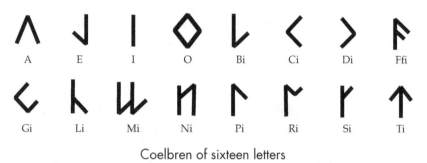

Coelbren of sixteen letters

Continuing with the traditional history, the Coelbren alphabet was nearly forgotten after the Roman conquest of Britain, when writing with ink on parchment replaced writing with a knife on wood, and the Roman alphabet came into common use. After the Roman legions departed and Christianity arrived, though, parchment became scarce and expensive but sticks remained plentiful and cheap, and so the older form of writing became a more practical option again. The famous bards Talhaiarn and Taliesin, who lived around the time of King Arthur, revived the Coelbren and added two new letters—again, the documents disagree as to which those were, but the most likely candidates are H and W.

17th and 18th Coelbren

Later, another bard, Ithel the Tawny added two more, probably U and Y. The twenty-letter alphabet that resulted was considered in later years to express the complete set of primary sounds of the Welsh language.

19th and 20th Coelbren

Finally, in the time of King Hywel the Good, who reigned from 920 to 950, Geraint the Blue Bard added four more letters representing compound sounds that were absent in the old British language but are common in Welsh: Ch, Dd, F (pronounced V), and Ll (a sound that's not used in English, which is explained in the next chapter).

Chi   Ddi   Fi   Lli

Four compound Coelbren

After Geraint's time, many other compound letters were introduced, making a complete Coelbren of the Bards of forty-four letters. According to Iolo's account, though, the later letters were the creations of scholarly grammarians and weren't actually used to write with. The twenty-four-letter Coelbren of Geraint the Blue Bard was the standard version taught by Iolo, and this is the Coelbren alphabet used in this book.

The actual history of the Coelbren

Turn from the pages of *Barddas* to the records of actual history, and the trail of the Coelbren, once it passes Iolo Morganwg, vanishes into mist. Despite an assortment of claims made down the years, nobody has yet turned up anything written in the Coelbren that definitely dates from before Iolo's time. As already noted, scholars these days have finally gotten around to admitting that Iolo did have access to at least some scraps of lore and some old manuscripts that don't seem to have survived to the present, and it's just possible that the Coelbren alphabet, or something like it, was in one of his lost sources. That said, unless good evidence surfaces to show that this happened, it's most likely that the original source of the Coelbren was Iolo Morganwg's vivid imagination and his extensive reading in traditional lore from all over western Europe and the ancient world.

These latter sources had plenty of raw material that could have inspired the creation of a bardic alphabet. The Ogham, an archaic Irish alphabet composed of tally marks, was well known in the scholarly literature of his time—the first detailed scholarly account of Ogham in modern times was published in 1685.[26] The runes, the ancient alphabet of the Vikings, the Anglo-Saxons, and other Germanic peoples, were introduced to British readers by way of *Northern Antiquities*, Paul Henri Mallet's groundbreaking collection of Nordic lore, which first appeared in English translation in 1770.[27] Both these alphabets, like the Coelbren, were designed for cutting or scratching onto hard surfaces, rather than writing with ink on paper.

Iolo knew about the runes—he drew up tables comparing the Coelbren to runes among other ancient alphabets[28]—and he likely knew about the Ogham; certainly John Williams ab Ithel was able to compare the Coelbren to the Ogham in a learned aside in *Dosparth Ederyn Dafod Aur*.[29] Iolo also knew about another survival from earlier times, the Staffordshire clog almanacs, which are wooden sticks notched with various symbolic markings, and were used to keep track of the calendar of church festivals. It's possible, though not proven, that he may have known of the original source of the clog almanacs, the stave almanacs of Scandinavia, which were brought to Britain by the Vikings when they settled large portions of eastern England in the ninth century. The stave almanacs are sets of seven long flat pieces of wood carved with runic inscriptions representing the days of the lunar month.[30]

All of these influences may have guided his creation of the Coelbren alphabet. The traditional history of the Coelbren given in *Barddas* also has a straightforward source that was known to most educated people in Iolo's time: the legendary origins of the Greek alphabet.

Like the Coelbren, the Greek alphabet traditionally didn't come into being all at once. According to the Roman scholar Hyginus,[31] who probably wrote in the first century CE, seven Greek letters—α (alpha), o (omicron), υ (upsilon), ε (eta), ι (iota), β (beta), and τ (tau)—were invented by the three Fates, or alternatively by the god Hermes, after he watched the patterns made by the legs of cranes as they flew. Eleven more were invented by the ancient hero Palamedes son of Nauplius. Epicharmus of Sicily, a writer of comedies, added θ (theta) and χ (chi), and the famous poet Simonides of Ceos added four more letters, ω (omega), η (epsilon),

[26] O'Flaherty 1685.
[27] Mallet 1770.
[28] Constantine 2007, p. 106.
[29] Williams ab Ithel 1856, pp. 19–21
[30] Pennick 1989, p. 39.
[31] Hyginus 1960.

ζ (zeta), and ψ (psi), to complete the alphabet. All this is very reminiscent of the process by which the modern Coelbren came into being, as recounted in *Barddas*, and it's at least possible that Iolo had it in mind when he penned the accounts of the Coelbren's history.

And the meanings of the Coelbren letters, which derive from the sound each letter makes? Iolo could easily have drawn inspiration for this, too, from a specific literary source that was well known in his time. To understand that source and its impact on history and spirituality down through the centuries, though, we'll need to take a detour far in space and time from early nineteenth-century Wales.

Sound symbolism

The sun beats down from the clear blue sky of ancient Greece. In the shade of a courtyard in Athens, two men sit on a stone bench, deep in discussion. The topic reaches straight down to the roots of language itself: do words get their meaning in an arbitrary way, simply because people decide to use this set of sounds instead of that one to mean "horse," or any other thing? That's what one of the men, Hermogenes, thinks. Or do the words of human language have some direct link to their meaning that can be decoded in some way from the sounds? That's what the other man, Cratylus, believes.

The two of them are so wrapped up in their debate that some minutes pass before they notice that a third man is standing nearby, watching them with a smile on his wrinkled face. Their friend Socrates has come to visit them. They invite him to join the discussion … and with that, one of the great books of classical philosophy is off and running.

The scene just described is the setting for the dialogue titled *Cratylus*, one of the writings of the great Greek philosopher Plato. Like many of Plato's dialogues, *Cratylus* circles around a set of important issues without settling on any one solution. That was a deliberate strategy, because Plato was interested in teaching people to ask questions, rather than filling their heads with canned answers. In the process, he posed questions about the nature of language that still haven't been settled once and for all.

These days, to be sure, most linguists agree with Hermogenes that the vocal noises we call "words" take their meaning solely from habit. Defenders of this view point to the fact that words for the same thing in different languages very often have few or no sounds in common.

Consider, as just one example, the Welsh word *march*, the French word *cheval*, and the English word "horse," all of which mean the same animal. They also point to the way that words can change their meaning completely over time. The English word "black," for instance, originally stood for the color white—it's closely related to the French word *blanc*, which still means "white." These are strong arguments, and not easy to dismiss.

Those who agree with Cratylus, though, have arguments of their own, which start from the fact that within each language, certain sounds are used repeatedly in words of related meaning. For example, it's remarkable how many words in English that refer to movement begin with the letter R: think of "run," "roll," "ride," "race," "rush," "rocket," "road," and so on, to say nothing of words that don't begin with R but stress the sound, such as "arrow," "torrent," "swerve," and so forth. It's just as remarkable how many obscenities in English take hissing sounds like F and Sh and hard popping sounds like K and T, and slap one or the other on each end of a one-syllable word. That's also true of less profane insults—"jerk!"[32]—and also of impolite phrases such as "shut up!" "Be quiet" is more polite, and it sounds that way: more fluid, less like a slap across the face. ("Slap," by the way, is another good example: a word for a rude action, as of course are some swear words.)

An entire category of words are given the tongue-twisting label "onomatapoeia," because they sound like what they mean—the word "splash," for example, sounds like the noise made by splashing water, "hiss" sounds like a hiss, and so on. One common version of the theory Cratylus defended in Plato's dialogue, the theory of sound symbolism, suggests that every language started out that way in the beginning, as early humans came up with vocal noises that sounded like what they wanted to communicate. Pay close attention to the sounds of language, the theory of sound symbolism suggests, and you can work your way back through time to the original sources and meanings of language itself.

Whether or not the theory of sound symbolism is correct will probably never be known for sure—not unless somebody comes up with a time machine, at least, or some other way to listen in on our earliest human ancestors as they found their way to the astonishing miracle of

---

[32] Note that this word also contains the R of movement, and one of its meanings is a sudden motion.

spoken language. The point that's relevant to the Coelbren is that if you want letters to have meanings as well as sounds, for whatever purpose, sound symbolism is one way to go about it.

It's not the only way, or even the most common. Most of the world's writing systems started out as simplified pictures. Our letter A, for example, began its career as a drawing of the head of an ox—it's been turned upside down over the centuries, and if you turn it back over it's easier to see the resemblance—and the sound it stands for is the first sound in *'alif*, the ancient Phoenician word for "ox." Many writing systems that give meaning to individual letters look back to the original pictures for the meaning, or simply use words that begin with the right letter: in the Irish Ogham alphabet, for example, the letter ⊨, Luis, relates symbolically to gray (in old Irish, *liath*) among colors, the duck (*lachu*) among birds, and so on.

Certain writing systems, however, use sound symbolism instead of picture symbolism for the same purpose. In Japan, the spiritual science of *kotodama*—literally, "word-soul"—is based on the symbolic meanings of each of the five vowel and ten consonant sounds of the Japanese language.[33] In central Europe, German-speaking mystics and occultists have developed their own system of sound symbolism based on the sound values of the German language.[34] Then, of course, there is the Coelbren, which makes use of an extremely detailed system of sound symbolism that relies partly on the vocal habits of the Welsh language, partly on the nature of the sounds themselves, and partly on the shapes made by the human mouth in producing those sounds. That system of sound symbolism is covered in detail in Chapter Three of this book.

Exactly where Iolo got the idea of using sound symbolism as the key to the meaning of the Coelbren may never be known for certain, but one obvious possibility is that he picked it up from the *Cratylus*, the same dialogue of Plato's that was cited above. Thomas Taylor, the great English Platonist, published an English translation of the *Cratylus* in 1793. Iolo, as already noted, was in London from 1791 to 1795, and moved in many of the same social circles as Taylor. Whether or not they

---

[33] There is very little in English on *kotodama*. See Gleason 1995, pp. 54–72, and Kushi 1979, pp. 124–128, for helpful overviews.
[34] Bardon 1971 and Lomer 1997, pp. 118–122, are accessible introductions in English.

ever met, Iolo could hardly have missed hearing about Taylor's translations, and one lively conversation that referenced the *Cratylus* could have been enough to send Iolo chasing after a copy.

For that matter, the evidence currently available doesn't show whether the sound symbolism of the Coelbren was Iolo's invention, or was introduced after his time by one of the bards who inherited his legacy. Some later student of Iolo's lore—quite possibly John Williams ab Ithel, who put a detailed description of the Coelbren's meanings in his translation of *Dosparth Ederyn Dafod Aur*—could have read the discussion of sound symbolism in the *Cratylus* and seen how it could be applied to the Coelbren of the Bards.

The practicalities of the Coelbren

The symbolic dimensions of the Coelbren don't exhaust their uses, though. As mentioned earlier in this chapter, they were also used, like any other alphabet, to write with. A number of Welsh poems written in the Coelbren, as mentioned earlier, still survive in museums in Wales. The only thing that sets them apart from other nineteenth-century Welsh poetic manuscripts is that they aren't written with ink on paper; they're written on squared wooden sticks with a knife.

According to *Barddas*, as already noted, this was the original medium of writing among the ancient Celts. If this idea was Iolo's invention, it was an inspired guess, because the Ogham and the runes—the two native scripts from northwestern Europe that are known to be authentic—were used in exactly this way, and show it in the forms of their letters, just as the Coelbren does.

The history of the Coelbren in *Barddas* has it that writing with ink on parchment was standard whenever parchment and other writing supplies were cheap and readily available. The troubled history of the British Isles, though, saw to it that there were times when wood and a sharp knife were much easier to come by. We've already seen that after the Romans pulled out of Britain in the fourth century CE, and the ancestors of the Welsh struggled against Saxon invaders, the old habit of writing on wood was supposed to have come back into use because parchment was scarce and costly. The same thing happened, according to *Barddas*, when Owain Glyndwr tried to liberate Wales from the English in the fifteenth century, and the English retaliation included an embargo on imports of writing materials to Wales.

Sensibly enough—after all, no one knew whether troubles of the same sort might happen again—the Welsh bards were charged with the task of preserving the practical details of using the Coelbren for ordinary writing, and *Barddas* and a few other bardic writings from Wales cover the process at quite some length. Branches of suitable trees were gathered in winter, before the sap rose. Hazel was the easiest wood to use for writing purposes, oak was the most enduring, and willow, alder, birch, plum, hawthorn, and apple were also used; but the bards preferred rowan, partly because the wood resists rot, partly because it has the traditional power to drive away evil spirits and enchantments, and partly in commemoration of the original three rowan staves on which Einigan the Giant carved all the wisdom of the world.

Whatever wood was chosen, clean straight branches two to three inches in diameter were cut into rods the length of a cubit (around 18 inches); each rod had the bark peeled off it and was then split lengthwise, and the halves split again. This yielded four long thin billets of wood, which were allowed to dry. The wood was then planed with a knife so that each billet had a square cross section and four flat sides, each about half an inch wide. The corners were trimmed down by a tenth of an inch or so, to keep the cuts made on one side from crossing onto another. The ebill, as the resulting stick was called, was then ready for use.

Cutting the letters into an ebill took the same skill and attention as any other kind of calligraphy. "And on this stave or ebill the letters are cut with a knife," according to *Barddas*,[35] "in small grooves the thickness of a leaf or small straw in depth, and as wide as a slender stalk of hay. Let every groove be cut fair and clear in its cutting." When a bard wanted to make what he was writing easier to read than ordinary knife-cut grooves could manage, a plant-based dye such as woad was rubbed across the face of the ebill before letters were carved into it, so that the letters stood out pale against a colored surface. Once carved, the ebill could be warmed, smeared with beeswax, and lightly roasted to make the wax penetrate the wood, as a further protection against decay.

A single ebill could hold four lines of poetry or an equivalent amount of prose. Each side was marked on one end so that readers could tell the order in which to read the sides. If a text required more than one ebill, they could be pierced at both ends with an iron auger heated in the fire,

---

[35] Williams ab Ithel 2004, p. 145.

and strung together on two strong cords, or inserted into a wooden frame that was lashed together at top and bottom. A frame of this sort, called a peithynen, normally held ten ebillion, or forty writing surfaces, enough for a substantial poem or a short tale; some frames are said to have held up to thirty ebillion, or 120 writing surfaces.

No peithynen survives from before Iolo's time, though it's fair to note that neither the climate nor the history of Wales are well suited to the preservation of fragile wooden objects tarred with the memories of a troubled past. For most of a century after Iolo's death, though, peithynenau were a common sight at bardic events in Wales and elsewhere. (For that matter, the same National Museum of Wales website mentioned earlier in this chapter has a photo of a peithynen bearing a poem commemorating Iolo Morganwg—an interesting contrast with the same website's claim that the Coelbren is a "false alphabet.")

Ebillion carved with a knife were said to be the most common medium for the bardic alphabet, but *Barddas* has it that certain other media were used as well. In the time of Llyr Llediaith, the father of Bran the Blessed of *Mabinogion* fame, bards were said to have devised a system in which heated iron stamps were used to burn the Coelbren letters into wood. (If this story has any historical validity, that process would count as one of the earliest forms of printing.) There were also small ebillion, the size of a finger, which were used by the bards to communicate their secret teachings; there were wooden cubes like dice, which had a letter carved onto each face, so that four of these cubes comprised the alphabet of twenty-four letters; and there were small pieces of wood with individual letters on them. The bardic literature claims that these latter two were used by bards for secret communication, but there's at least one other likely use for them, which will be discussed in Chapter Four of this book.

The same symbols could also be scratched onto stone with a sharp steel point. In this context they were called Coelfaen rather than Coelbren (from *maen*, "stone," in place of *pren*, "wood"). Stones bearing individual letters or the "marks of mystery," whatever those may have been, filled the same roles as the small ebillion and individually lettered pieces of wood mentioned above. On a larger scale, according to *Barddas*, the laws of King Hywel the Good were originally written on pieces of slate that lined the walls of his royal hall, and King Arthur had the laws of the Round Table and the praiseworthy deeds of its knights written on plates of tin and brass at his three principal courts in the towns of Caerleon, Celliwig, and Penrhyn. All this belongs to the legenday history of the Coelbren, but the fact remains that the Coelbren letters are useful whenever scratching or carving on a hard surface is a more convenient way of writing than using paper and ink.

Just at the moment, it seems unlikely that anyone will have to go back to writing on sticks with a knife any time soon—though I sometimes wonder how many people in the last years of Roman Britain assumed as a matter of course that their comfortable existence would go on forever. Even aside from that, though, the uses of the Coelbren aren't limited to the things that more ordinary forms of writing can do. The fourth chapter of this book will explore one of the most popular and enthusiastically practiced of those: the art of divination.

CHAPTER THREE

The letters of the Coelbren

ΛVⵃ<ꓩ⟩ᒐᛕ𐌓Oᒋ

> It was out of the knowledge and understanding of the vocal-
> ization of language and speech, by reason of the three princi-
> pal letters, that sixteen letters were formed, constructed from
> the primary columns, namely, the three principal letters in the
> form of rays of light. And it was thus that form and appearance
> could be imparted to every vocalization of language and speech,
> and to every primary sound, and symbolic forms of memory be
> made visible on wood and stone.
>
> —*Barddas*[36]

As explained in Chapter Two, the Coelbren alphabets Iolo Morganwg
taught to his bardic students range from the mysterious ten-letter
Abcedilros, which conceals the Secret of the Bards of the Isle of Britain,
to the thirty-eight letters used, or at least proposed, by finicky Welsh
grammarians. The twenty-four-letter alphabet of Geraint the Blue Bard,
which was traditionally established in the tenth century during the
reign of Hywel the Good, was the most common of these, and it's the
one that is used in this book.

---

[36] Williams ab Ithel 2004, p. 23.

Each letter of the Coelbren has certain traditional correspondences:

Name: The name of each Coelbren letter is the sound it makes. This should come as no surprise, given the importance of sound symbolism in the Coelbren tradition! Remember, when you read the names of the letters, that the vowels aren't pronounced the way they are in English—thus A, for example, is pronounced "Ah," not "Ay." Similarly, E is pronounced "Eh," I is pronounced "Ee," O is "Oh," W is "Oo" as in "pool," Y is sometimes "Ee" and sometimes the neutral vowel sound of the "e" in "tunnel" and "cheapen," and U is pronounced something like the German "ü" or the French "eu."[37]

The consonants are all pronounced with the vowel I following them: Bi, Ci, Di, and so on. Traditionally, when pronouncing the name of a consonant, the vowel wasn't given its full pronunciation "ee;" "the sound really emitted in the effort to express any idea," Williams ab Ithel noted, "seems to have been somewhat like the short obscure *e* before *r* in final syllables of English words."[38]

Some consonants have a different pronunciation in Welsh than they do in English. In Welsh, C is always hard as in "cat," never soft as in "cell"; G, likewise, is hard as in "get," not soft as in "gene." F is pronounced like the English letter V, while Ff has the same sound as English F. Dd is the soft "th" sound in "these clothes," not the hard sound in "thin cloth." Ch is the same sound you find in the name of the German composer Bach or that famous monster-haunted lake in Scotland, Loch Ness. Finally, there's Ll, which is legendarily difficult for English speakers to get right. It's pronounced more or less like "hl"; some instructions are given in the discussion of the letter Lli below, but those should be supplemented by finding a recording of a fluent Welsh speaker, online or elsewhere, and listening carefully to the way he or she pronounces the letter.[39]

---

[37] Round your lips as though you were going to say "Oo," and then try to say "Ee" instead, then relax your lips as far as you can without changing the sound significantly, and you'll be fairly close.

[38] Williams ab Ithel 1856, p. 14.

[39] More generally, all the sounds of Welsh are best learned either from a fluent native speaker, or from recordings or online sound files. There are many resources online, including Welsh language radio programs and language learning sites, which should be consulted by the student.

Welsh keyword: It so happens that many of the names of the Coelbren letters are also short words in Welsh. Where such keywords exist, they're helpful guides to the meanings of the letters whose names they share. For example, the Coelbren letter C has the name Ci— remember that this is pronounced "kee"—which is the ordinary Welsh word for "dog." The meanings of this letter include catching, holding, reaching for something, and the like; think of a dog taking hold of a stick in your hand and playfully refusing to let go of it, and you'll have a good basic sense of the energy of this letter.

Meaning: This is a brief summary of the traditional meaning of the letter, derived from the sound symbolism. Once you gain some experience with the Coelbren, you'll pick up an intuitive sense of what the individual letters communicate to you. Until then, the summary here will be useful as a reminder.

Sound symbolism: As explained in Chapter Two, this is the source of the Coelbren tradition, and it deserves careful study.[40] Whoever assigned meanings to the Coelbren letters—whether that was done by Iolo Morganwg himself, the medieval bards from whom he claimed the tradition descended, or the Welsh Druids of the first half of the nineteenth century, who took up Iolo's work where he left it and reworked his legacy into a living tradition—paid very close attention to the way the human mouth shapes sounds, and tried to reach back to the beginnings of human communication to find the natural meanings of the basic elements of speech. Whether or not that quest succeeded, the sound symbolism attached to the Coelbren letters is the basis of each letter's meaning and provides insights that will be crucial in divination.

Divinatory meaning: Finally, my experience casting Coelbren readings has revealed certain patterns of meaning common to each of the letters, and these are summarized here. As you cast and interpret readings yourself, you'll find your own personal understanding of each letter, which may or may not match what's given in this book. We'll discuss this further in Chapter Four.

---

[40] The notes by John Williams ab Ithel to the *Dosparth Edeyrn Davod Aur*, from which the sound symbolism in the following notes is derived, only cover the sixteen letters of the Coelbren of Beli ap Manogan—a, e, i, o, b, c, d, g, l, m, n, p, r, s, and t. I have given the remaining eight letters of the Coelbren of Geraint the Blue Bard their symbolism by applying the same principles to their respective sounds. Purists who prefer the traditional approach are welcome to use the Coelbren of sixteen letters instead.

Name: A
Welsh keyword: *a*, and
Meaning: Proceeding forward; continuation in the same state or condition, whether of motion, action, or rest.

Sound symbolism: Draw in a breath, and say the sound "Ah" aloud. If you pay attention to your mouth as you do this, you'll notice that the lips are open and relaxed, the tongue lying against the floor of your mouth, and the mouth itself without tension, so that the sound and the breath flow easily and steadily outwards. Thus the sound and the letter stand for continuity, spontaneity, and ease, a steady and relaxed condition of motion or rest.

Divinatory meaning: When this letter appears in a divination, it stands for this same quality of easy continuity. If the letter appears in a position that represents you, the advice it offers is to keep on doing what you've been doing, and follow through in the direction you've already started going; if it represents another person for whom you are casting a reading, the same advice applies. If it appears in a position that represents someone or something else, it predicts that whoever or whatever it is will continue to have the same role as it's had up to this point; you don't need to worry that he, she, or it will suddenly change direction or do something you don't expect. If it appears in a position representing the whole situation, it predicts smooth sailing in general. Unless most of the other letters in the reading say otherwise, this is usually an indication of success.

Name: E
Welsh keyword: The prefix *e-*, which reverses the meaning of a word—for example, *ang* means "narrow," but *eang* means "wide."

Meaning: Motion checked, interrupted, or broken, an indirect, negative, or distorted condition.

Sound symbolism: Again draw in a breath, make the sound "Ah" aloud, and then change to "Eh." Feel how your tongue arches up and your mouth tenses to restrict the flow of air through your mouth. Where the Coelbren letter A represents continuity, spontaneity, and ease, the letter E represents the opposite of this; it expresses stoppage and interruption, a need to change direction or continue in an indirect or roundabout fashion.

Divinatory meaning: When this letter appears in a reading, it means that things are not going to continue in the way they appear to be going now. If the letter is in a position that represents you, it means that you will have to change direction or even, if the other letters in the reading support this interpretation, give up entirely on the project you have in mind. If it represents someone or something in your life, that person or thing will act as an obstacle, forcing you to reconsider your approach and try something different. Whenever it appears in a reading, it shows that change is needed, and the other letters in the reading will help you determine what has to change and how you can redirect your efforts to achieve what you want out of the situation.

Name: I
Welsh keyword: *i*, into

Meaning: The movement of a thing to its proper place, being or becoming a part of a whole, approach, applicability, subordination.

Sound symbolism: Make the sound "Eee" and pay attention to the shape of your mouth and the movement of your tongue. Feel how the mouth tightens and the tongue rises to direct the breath along a very narrow passage along your palate, while the tip of the tongue drops behind the teeth. The way the mouth draws together around the sound gives it its meaning, which is going into a place or relationship, approaching, fitting in, becoming part of something, belonging to something.

Divinatory meaning: When this letter appears in a reading, it indicates movement toward or into something—whether this is a good thing or not depends partly on the position the letter has in the reading, and partly on the nature of the question. If it turns up in an appropriate position in a reading about getting a job, for example, it's a strong indication that your application will be accepted; if it appears in a reading about leaving a relationship, it likely means that you will be better off staying put. In a position that represents you, or another person for whom you are casting a reading, it indicates that going onward into whatever is under discussion is your best, or even your only choice. In a position that represents someone or something other than you, the person or thing it represents will be entering your life.

Name: O
Welsh keyword: *o*, from

Meaning: Movement outward or away from, departure, rejection or projection, casting or putting forth.

Sound symbolism: Make the sound "Oh" and, once again, pay attention to the shape of your mouth and the position of your tongue. If you go back and forth between "Oh" and "Eee," you'll notice that the two positions are exactly opposite—to say "Oh," you draw your tongue back, open up your mouth, and round your lips. The sound symbolism of this letter is therefore the opposite of I: it means going out of a place or relationship, departing, separating from something, giving up or getting rid of something.

Divinatory meaning: When this letter appears in a reading, it indicates movement away from or out of something—again, whether this is a good thing or not depends on the position of the letter in the reading and the question that's been asked. If it represents you, or another person for whom you are casting a reading, it may be telling you it's time to leave a situation that's passed its pull date; it may mean that the situation is about to end and leave you to do something else with your life; or it may mean that you will be leaving the situation whether you want to do so or not. If it represents something or someone in your life, similarly, that thing or person will be going away in one sense or another.

V Name: W
Welsh keyword: (none)

Meaning: Sorting or distributing things into different classes or categories, discrimination, divergence, choosing.

Sound symbolism: Make the sound "Ah" and then slowly shift to the sound "Ooo," paying close attention to the movements of your lips and tongue. Notice the way the lips tighten into a narrow circle while the tongue draws back, away from the lips and the opening. This divergence gives the letter W its sound symbolism of dividing, sorting out, or making a choice between different alternatives.

Divinatory meaning: When this letter appears in a reading, it indicates a point of decision, at which some things will go one way and some will go a different way. If the letter represents you, or another person for whom you are casting a reading, it may be telling you that it's time to make a choice between alternatives, or to pay closer attention to the various options; if it represents someone or something else, it may mean that someone else will make a decision that affects you, or that some other kind of division or sorting out will be taking place. At its best, this letter indicates an abundance of possibilities, but it can also warn of a parting of the ways where you will have to make your choice and live with it.

Y Name: Y
Welsh keyword: *y*, the

Meaning: A state or condition of balance or suspension, neutrality, pause, impartiality or uninvolvement.

Sound symbolism: The Welsh letter Y has two sounds, one of them like the English "ee" as in "see," which is used in the last syllable of words or in most words of only one syllable, the other like the English unstressed "e" as in the last syllable of "camel," which is used everywhere else. (For example, *dyn*, "man," is pronounced "deen," but *dynion*, "men," is pronounced "duh-NEE-on.") The latter is the sound that gives this letter its symbolism. Make the sound and notice that your mouth is held in a neutral position, neither entirely open nor entirely closed, with no part of the mouth narrower or tighter than any other.

Divinatory meaning: When this letter appears in a reading, it indicates that this is not the time to make a decision or take action. If the letter is in a position that represents you, the advice it gives is to wait, and put off any definite action for the time being; if it represents another person for whom you are casting the reading, the same advice applies. If it represents something or someone else, you can expect delays, uncertainties, or simply complete uninvolvement or lack of interest on the part of other people involved. This can be frustrating if it represents something that you want, but remember that it can also represent something that you don't want—in which case you don't have to worry about it happening immediately or, depending on the other letters in the reading, at all.

Y Name: U
Welsh keyword: (none)

Meaning: Wholeness, completeness, unity, the background or context in which other things or actions have their place.

Sound symbolism: In the southern parts of Wales this letter is pronounced like I, but in the northern part of the principality it has a sound rarely heard in English. To make it, purse your lips as though you were going to make the sound "Ooh," and then without changing the shape of your mouth, try to say "Eee" instead. Now relax your lips slowly, and go as far as you can without changing the sound. You'll find, when you reach that point, that your mouth is held gently open and your lips are rounded and slightly tensed. Feel the circles into which your mouth is drawn; these are symbols of wholeness and completion, and give the letter its meaning.

Divinatory meaning: When this letter appears in a reading, it indicates that the situation is either already complete or is moving toward completion on its own, no matter what you do or don't do. If it represents you, it reminds you that you are part of a bigger picture than you may realize, and outside forces will have a larger impact on the outcome than anything you do or don't do. If it represents someone or something else, it suggests that one way or another, you (or another person for whom you are casting the reading) may not be able to do much to influence that part of the picture. It may also indicate that the question you have asked is too incomplete or too simplistic to be answered in any straightforward way.

Name: Bi
Welsh keyword: *bi*, will be
Meaning: The being of any thing in a quiescent state, a condition or state of being, mere existence, perception.

Sound symbolism: Close your mouth, relax it, and then say the name of the letter, "Bi." It takes less movement of the mouth to produce this sound than any other consonant in the Coelbren. It's for this reason, according to the traditional lore, that this sound became the symbol of simple existence, of a condition or state of being, and of what is.

Divinatory meaning: When this letter appears in a reading, it means that things are what they are, and will not change by themselves. If it shows up in a position that represents you, it means that whatever part of yourself or your life you're asking about will keep on doing what it's been doing and being what it's been being. The same meaning also applies, of course, if you're casting a reading for another person and this letter appears in a position representing that person. If it shows up in a position that represents someone or something else in your life, the same rule applies: that person or thing isn't about to change. Depending on the other letters in the reading, this letter may mean that things aren't going to change until and unless you change them—or it may mean that things aren't going to change no matter what you do, and you probably need to learn to live with that.

Name: Ci
Welsh keyword: *ci*, dog
Meaning: Holding, containing, comprehending, reaching or extension toward a thing, catching, attaining and apprehending.

Sound symbolism: Say the name of the letter Ci—again, remember that this sounds like "kee," not "see"! Feel the way the middle of the tongue arches up against the roof of the mouth, and forces the breath to push through against resistance. This gives the letter its sound symbolism of catching and holding, and thus of attempting to catch, reaching outwards, touching, and attaining.

Divinatory meaning: When this letter appears in a reading, it indicates getting and holding. If you're casting a reading about whether you or another person can get something, such as a job or a romantic partner, the answer this letter gives is yes; if the question is whether you or another person can avoid getting something, such as an illness, the answer in that case is no! In a different position, or in response to a different kind of question, it can mean that something is going to catch you or another person, for good or ill. More broadly, it represents reaching or moving toward something; depending on the place in the reading where it appears, it can offer advice—"move toward this," or give a warning—"this is coming toward you," but in any case, the common theme of reaching and grasping remains the same.

> **Name:** Di
> **Welsh keyword:** *di*, without

Meaning: Expanding, unfolding, laying open, distribution and division, the opposite of Ci.

Sound symbolism: Say the name of the letter Di and pay attention to the position of the tongue as its forward part lies flat against the roof of the mouth, then suddenly opens to make the sound. That opening movement gives the letter its sound symbolism of releasing, unfolding, spreading out, letting go, dividing and distributing.

Divinatory meaning: When this letter appears in a reading, it indicates letting go and giving away. If it appears in a position that represents you or another person for whom you are casting a reading, it shows that it's time for you or the other person to let go of something. If the purpose of the reading is to find out if you can get something, the answer is therefore "no"—modified, of course, by the other letters in the reading—while if the issue under discussion is whether you can get over something or get out of something, the answer is "yes." If this letter represents another person, that person will be releasing or giving away whatever is under discussion, and if it represents something desired by many people, it will be divided and distributed among them.

Name: Ffi
Welsh keyword: (none)
Meaning: Causation, impulsion, setting a thing or action in motion, the source or initial impetus of change or activity.

Sound symbolism: The Welsh letter Ff—even though it's written with two symbols, this counts as a single letter in Welsh—is pronounced like the English letter F (F in Welsh has the same sound as the English letter V). Say the name of the letter Ffi, and notice the way that the air is forced out through the narrow gap between your lower lip and your teeth, if you pronounce the Ff sound one common way, or between your upper and lower lips, if you pronounce it the other common way. This forcing of the air gives the letter its sound symbolism of causing something or making something move.

Divinatory meaning: When this letter appears in a reading, it indicates that things are going to have to be set in motion—they won't change unless something happens to make them change. If the letter appears in a position that represents you, it means that nothing is going to happen unless you do something, and if you're doing a reading for another person, that person should take the same advice. If it represents one of the other people involved in the situation about which you're casting the reading, that person is pushing the situation ahead. If it represents a thing rather than a person, that thing, rather than a person, is driving the situation onward. In every situation when this letter appears, it points to the cause or source of whatever the reading is about.

Name: Gi
Welsh keyword: *gi*, tendon
Meaning: Attachment, cohesion, appetite, desire, and also compensation and mutual reaction of things on each other.

Sound symbolism: Say the name of the letter Gi—remember that the G is hard, as in "get," not soft as in "gene"—and notice the position and movement of your mouth and tongue as you say it. The initial position is the same one that's used for the letter Ci, but the movement and sound are different; instead of the sudden burst of air forcing its way past the upraised middle of the tongue, the movement is gentler and the breath less explosive. This gives the letter its sound symbolism, which is a gentler form of Ci—instead of catching and holding, Gi represents attachment, cohesion, and compensation.

Divinatory meaning: When this letter appears in a reading, it indicates that the various elements of the situation are closely connected to one another, so that changing one thing will change everything else. If it appears in a position representing you, or another person for whom you're casting a reading, it suggests that any attempt to make things happen will set off a cascade of changes with results you will not be able to predict. This doesn't necessarily mean that doing so is a bad idea, just that you need to be prepared for the unexpected! If it appears in a position indicating another person, it suggests that this person is connected to the situation in ways that go beyond the obvious, and if it indicates something other than a person, whatever happens to that thing will have consequences that you may not yet suspect.

Name: Hi
Welsh keyword: *hi*, she
Meaning: Generation, abundance, fertility, nurturance and support, response favorable to an external cause or stimulus.

Sound symbolism: Speak the name of the letter Hi—that's not pronounced like the short version of "Hello" in English, remember, but like "Hee." Draw out the H sound, and pay attention to the position of your tongue and mouth as you say it. Notice the way that the tongue and palate form a narrow open space. To a less prudish age than ours, the shape the mouth forms in this position immediately suggested a vagina, and thus the feminine and fertility-oriented symbolism of this letter.

Divinatory meaning: When this letter appears in a reading, it is a generally positive sign in most questions. If it appears in a position representing you or another person for whom you are casting a reading, it encourages a receptive and favorable approach to whatever events or actions the reading discusses. If it appears in a position that represents another person or the situation in general, it predicts that the person or situation will be receptive to whatever you (or the person for whom you're casting a reading) are trying to do. In questions involving pregnancy and childbirth, for obvious reasons, it is a very favorable omen!

Name: Li
Welsh keyword: (none)
Meaning: Flow, softness, smoothness, lightness, open space, solution or evanescence, movement without effort, as gliding.

Sound symbolism: L is an uncommon sound in Welsh—Ll, which counts as a different letter and represents a sound that doesn't occur in English, is heard much more often—but it gets used now and then, especially when a word beginning with Ll is affected by certain details of Welsh grammar. Speak the name of the letter Li, drawing out the "L" sound, and pay attention to the way you hold your tongue and mouth. Depending on where you grew up, when you say Li, the breath will flow out around one or both sides of your tongue. The fluid way the breath moves is the source of this letter's sound symbolism.

Divinatory meaning: When this letter appears in a reading, it indicates that the situation is flowing smoothly, and no effort is required to make it proceed. If the letter appears in a position that represents you or another person for whom you are casting a reading, it offers specific advice: it's a good time to let things go the way they want to go, rather than trying to make them do what you think you want them to do. If it appears in a position representing other people or things, they are out of your control, and you simply have to accept that they're going to do what they're going to do. Unless other letters in the reading suggest otherwise, though, this is usually a favorable omen, suggesting that if things are allowed to go their own way, you or the person for whom you're casting the reading will be happy with the result.

Name: Mi
Welsh keyword: *mi*, I
Meaning: Comprehending, embracing, or surrounding; enclosure or capacity, inclusion within something; large or complex.

Sound symbolism: Speak the name of this letter aloud, drawing out the M sound. Notice the way that the mouth stays entirely closed and the cheeks move slightly outward, as though to suggest the idea of holding or enclosing. This gives the letter Mi its sound symbolism of containing and embracing, and also of great size or complexity and of being included.

Divinatory meaning: When this letter appears in a reading, it indicates that there is more going on in the subject of the divination than you realize, and attention to the big picture is crucial. When it appears in a position that represents you, or another person for whom you are casting a reading, it suggests that whatever you do (or that person does) will affect, and be affected by, many other people and things; depending on the other letters in the reading, it may also indicate that you (or the other person) can accomplish your goals only as part of a group, or that you or the other person are limited by the choices other people make. When it appears in a position that represents some other person or thing, it warns that there is much more going on with that person or thing than you realize. More generally, when this letter appears anywhere in a reading, it can also mean that the situation is much larger or more complex than it seems.

Name: Ni
Welsh keyword: *ni,* not[41]
Meaning: Distinguishing or identifying something; an individual object or subject; something new, simple, distinguished, or small.

Sound symbolism: Speak the name of this letter aloud, drawing out the N sound. Notice how the tongue presses forward against the back of the teeth, as though pointing at something. This gives the letter its sound symbolism—it is as though you were pointing at something, saying, "Look at that!" John Williams ab Ithel's essay on the Coelbren's sound symbolism notes that Ni, "Look" or "Lo there!" is naturally answered by Mi, "I observe, I comprehend."[42]

Divinatory meaning: When this letter appears in a reading, it indicates that whatever it represents is the key to the entire situation. As the sound symbolism suggests, the letter is pointing toward something, saying, "Look there!" If it appears in a position that represents you, it tells you that your own choices and actions are the key to the entire situation; if you are casting a reading for someone else and the letter appears in a place representing that person, the same rule applies. If it represents some other person or thing, the resolution of the situation depends on that person or thing alone. More generally, this letter can also mean that the situation is much smaller or less complex than it appears.

Name: Pi
Welsh keyword: *pi,* magpie
Meaning: Pushing, penetrating, springing or putting forth; a protrusion or prominence, sharpness, convexity.

---

[41] Fans of the Monty Python comic troupe who want to know whether this letter has any reference to a famous scene in *Monty Python and the Holy Grail* should consult a shrubber, or possibly an enchanter named Tim.
[42] Williams ab Ithel 1856, p. 17.

Sound symbolism: Speak the name of the letter Pi aloud, and feel the way that the breath presses against the lips until it pushes its way through. This sudden breakthrough of the breath gives the letter its sound symbolism of pushing, penetrating, and thrusting through.

Divinatory meaning: When this letter appears in a reading, it indicates that sudden change is in the offing, for good or ill. Something is breaking through, or will break through, or has broken through—the nature of the question and the position in which the letter appears will tell you which of these is the case. If it appears in a position representing you, or another person for whom you're casting a reading, it means that you or that person will be responsible for the breakthrough; if it represents another person or thing, then that's where the breakthrough will happen. The other letters in the reading will reveal what will happen as a result of the sudden change.

Name: Ri
Welsh keyword: *rhi*, king
Meaning: Force, prevalence, or superiority; an action performed by main strength; excess, tearing or breaking, causing damage.

Sound symbolism: In Welsh, R is rolled or trilled in much the same way that it is in Scotland; some English speakers have trouble pronouncing the letter this way. If you can do so, speak the name of the letter Ri aloud, rolling the R sound and drawing it out. Notice the way that the tip of the tongue vibrates against the front of the palate, driven up and down by the force of the breath. This gives Ri its sound symbolism of force, violence, and domination. In Williams ab Ithel's essay on the Coelbren, Ri and Li are presented as opposites.[43]

Divinatory meaning: When this letter appears in a reading, it indicates that the situation has passed the point at which subtle or gentle measures will do the job. If it appears in a position that represents you, it suggests that vigorous action on your part will be needed to bring things to the desired conclusion, but unless it is accompanied by very unfortunate letters, it also indicates that you have the strength to finish the job. If it represents another person for whom you're casting a reading, the same advice applies to that person. If it appears in a position that indicates another person or thing, though, this letter is usually a

---

[43] Williams ab Ithel 1856, p. 18.

bad sign, and indicates that someone or something else has more power over the situation than you do, and can be expected to use that strength in a forceful manner.

Name: Si
Welsh keyword: *si*, murmur
Meaning: Inferiority, secrecy, privacy; a secret or private knowledge or indication; insinuation, indirect action.

Sound symbolism: Say the name of the letter Si aloud, drawing out the S sound. Pay attention to the way that the tip of the tongue bends down and the air sneaks out between the tongue and the palate. The hissing sound, like a whisper or a sudden warning to be silent, gives the letter Si its sound symbolism of secrecy, insinuation, and privacy, and from these meanings unfolds the secondary meaning of weakness and indirect action.

Divinatory meaning: When this letter appears in a reading, it indicates that secrecy, indirect action, and circumspection are crucial factors of the situation. If it appears in a position that represents you, it means that you don't have enough power over the situation to take direct action, and therefore will have to use indirect means and avoid attracting notice in order to bring about the desired results. If it appears in the same position in a reading you're casting for another person, it very often means that the other person has not told you everything you need to know about the situation! If it appears in a position that represents someone or something else, there are hidden factors at work in the situation; the other letters in the reading will tell you whether you or the person for whom you're casting the reading will be able to find out what's really going on.

Name: Ti
Welsh keyword: (none)
Meaning: Tension, drawing, or straining; stretching or drawing out; bringing to an end; confinement or termination.

Sound symbolism: Speak the name of the letter Ti aloud. Notice the sudden break as the tongue moves down from the front of the palate, behind the teeth, and the breath bursts forward. This gives the letter its sound symbolism of tensing, confining, and limiting, and thus of the closing or termination of a process.

Divinatory meaning: When this letter appears in a reading, it indicates that something is coming to an end. If it appears in a position that represents you or another person for whom you are casting a reading, it very often means that the situation has gone too far for any action of yours (or the other person's) to change; if it appears in a position representing another person or thing, that person or thing may be leaving soon, and if it appears in a position representing a situation—for example, a job or a relationship—that situation will not last long. Stress and tension, which so often accompany the arrival of endings, are also very often indicated by this letter.

Name: Ddi
Welsh keyword: (none)
Meaning: Realm, extent, or field of action; territory; boundary, surface, or interface marking the limit of a given force or influence.

Sound symbolism: The Welsh letter Dd, as mentioned earlier in this book, has the sound of "th" as in the English phrase "these clothes," not as in "thin cloth." Speak the letter Ddi aloud, stretching out the Dd sound. Feel the way that your tongue presses close to your teeth and arches downward behind, enclosing and defining an empty space. This gives the letter its sound symbolism of a realm or territory, and from this comes the secondary sense of boundary, surface, or furthest extent of a force or an influence.

Divinatory meaning: When this letter appears in a reading, it indicates the presence of a boundary that you may not be able to cross. If it appears in a position representing you, it indicates that your ability to affect the situation will only extend so far, and very often advises you to pay attention to the difference between what you can influence and what you can't, and focus on what you can actually do something about; if it represents another person for whom you're casting a reading, the same advice applies. If it appears in a position that represents someone or something else, it may mean that this person or thing is out of your reach, or alternatively that he, she, or it has only a limited ability to affect the situation—the question the reading is meant to answer, and the other letters in the reading, will tell you which of these is the case.

Name: Lli
Welsh keyword: *lli*, flood
Meaning: Turbulence, confusion, and disruption; difficulty in proceeding; obstacles, solidity, movement requires effort.

Sound symbolism: The sound of the Welsh letter Lli isn't used in English, though it's found in some languages besides Welsh.[44] The easiest way for most English speakers to learn how to say it is, first, to put your mouth in position to say the sound of the letter L, and then, without moving your mouth, try to say H instead. (Listening to a good recording of a native Welsh speaker is the next step, and will help you get the details right.) Speak the name of the letter Lli as best you can, and pay attention to the way the breath flows around the side of your tongue in a rough, turbulent manner. This gives the letter its sound symbolism of turbulence, disruption, and difficulty.

Divinatory meaning: When this letter appears in a reading, it indicates that troubles and obstacles are ahead. If it appears in a position that indicates you, or another person for whom you're casting a reading, expect a difficult time accomplishing anything—the other letters in the reading will tell you what will cause the trouble. If it appears in a position that represents some other person, that person will be having a hard time, and if it represents a thing, there will be trouble over that thing. Depending on the letters that appear with it, it may also simply indicate that a lot of things will be happening very fast and you will find it hard to stay on track and avoid getting confused.

Name: Fi

Welsh keyword: *fe,* he

Meaning: Protection, limitation, discipline, establishment or maintenance of order; response unfavorable to an external cause or stimulus.

Sound symbolism: The Welsh letter F is pronounced like the English letter V. Speak the name of the letter Fi, drawing out the V sound, and notice the position your mouth takes in order to produce the sound, with the lower lip pressed against the upper teeth and the upper lip raised to bare the teeth, the way an animal bares its teeth in a snarl. This gives the letter its sound symbolism of protection, guardianship, and hostility to outside influences.

---

[44] The city of Seattle, in Washington State, was named after a Native American chieftain, and in the Lushootseed Salish language that Chief Seattle spoke, the final sound of his name is the same as the Welsh Ll. (His name would be spelled Seall in Welsh.) The same sound is common in the languages of most of the First Nations of the northwest coast of North America; for example, the first sound in the name of the Tlingit tribe is the same as the Welsh Ll.

Divinatory meaning: When this letter appears in a reading, it is a generally negative sign in most questions. If it appears in a position that represents you or another person for whom you are casting a reading, it encourages a guarded and cautious attitude to whatever events or actions the reading discusses. If it appears in a position that represents another person or the situation in general, it predicts that the person or situation will be opposed to whatever you (or the person for whom you're casting a reading) are trying to do. Whenever it appears, it is a warning of potential trouble, and advises that firm boundaries and a wary attitude are essential.

K **Name:** Chi
Welsh keyword: (none)
Meaning: Conflict, opposition, obstacle; mutual interference between two or more contending forces or things.

Sound symbolism: The Welsh letter Ch, as already noted, is pronounced as in the name of the composer Bach or in Loch Ness, not as in "cheese." Say the name of the letter Chi aloud, drawing out the Ch sound, and notice how the middle of the tongue arches up, as it does in the letter Ci. With Chi, though, in place of the clear Ci sound, the air comes through roughly, as though struggling to force its way out. This gives the letter its sound symbolism of conflict, interference, and a struggle against obstacles.

Divinatory meaning: When this letter appears in a reading, it indicates that some kind of struggle is in the offing. When it appears in a position that represents you, or another person for whom you're casting a reading, it shows that you or the other person will have to contend with obstacles or opposition to achieve anything worthwhile. When it appears in a position that represents someone or something else, that person or thing is going to be facing a struggle. This letter differs from Lli in that it doesn't just predict complications, confusion, and difficulty; active opposition of some kind is involved. Whether that opposition comes from a specific person, from impersonal forces, or from the sheer inertia of the situation, you are in for a fight.

CHAPTER FOUR

Coelbren divination

ᚾᛚᚲᛃᛞᛁᚲᚱᛟᚱ

> The mysteries of the Bards, that is to say, the secret Coelbrens, are small ebillion, a finger long, having notches ... They are called the Charms of the Bards, or Bardic Mystery. Secret Coelfains are similar, made of small stones bearing the marks of mystery; and it is by disposing them, according to the arrangement and art of the Secret, that necessary sciences are demonstrated.
>
> —*Barddas*[45]

A symbolic alphabet such as the Coelbren of the Bards can be used for many different purposes and in many different ways. Nowadays, though, their most common use is as a tool for divination. Since the publication of Ralph Blum's *The Book of Runes* in 1982, the various futharks (runic alphabets) have come into widespread use in divination, and not only among believers in the Norse gods and goddesses. Similarly, Colin and Beth Murray's *The Celtic Tree Oracle* introduced the old Irish Ogham alphabet as a divinatory oracle to students of traditional Celtic spirituality and a wider audience as well.

---

[45] Williams ab Ithel 2004, p. 155.

The Coelbren of the Bards is equally well suited to that use. What's more, it may have been a means of divination from the beginning of its documented history. Though I have not been able to find any references to Coelbren divination in Iolo's writings or those of his students and heirs, one crucial clue survives in the name of the alphabet itself.

The second half of the term Coelbren, as already noted, comes from the Welsh word *pren*, "tree," "timber," or "wood." The first half comes from the word *coel*, which in modern Welsh means "belief," "trust," or "credit." In old Welsh, though, *coel* had a different and more specific meaning: "omen."[46] A Coelbren is thus literally an "omen stick," and a Coelfaen—a stone marked with one of the letters of the bardic alphabet—is an "omen stone." Iolo was far too capable a student of medieval Welsh—and far too skilled a forger—to have missed this, and it seems improbable that he would have given his alphabet a name likely to raise eyebrows among other scholars if he did not intend it to be used for casting omens, or as we now say, divination.

If the Coelbren was used for divination in Iolo's time, as this suggests, no trace has apparently survived of the specific techniques that he and his students developed. Fortunately, enough work has been done with other divinatory oracles since his time that it's an easy matter to borrow appropriate methods from elsewhere and adapt them to use with the Coelbren.

That borrowing needs to be done with a certain amount of care, to be sure. Every oracle has its own "personality," expressed most clearly in the ways that it communicates meaning to diviners. The tarot, for example, encodes its meanings in complex visual images; the runes have simpler meanings tied up in concepts familiar to the ancient Germanic tribes that originated them—wealth, rain, journey, ice, sun, and so on; the Ogham fews (letters) are associated with trees and their traditional folklore, and so on.

The Coelbren is no exception to this rule, and the way it expresses its meanings is as distinct from each of the oracles just mentioned as they are from one another. The Coelbren is an oracle of flow and change. Each letter expresses a stage in a process: free flow or restriction, movement in or movement out, and so on through a range of transformations that expresses the possibilities of life and movement. At first glance, the meanings of the letters may seem vague to you, but if you think of them

---

[46] In modern Welsh, the word for "superstition" is still *coelgrefydd*, literally "belief in omens."

as qualities of motion or kinds of change, you'll soon learn that they express a great deal of very precise meaning.

Oracles also vary in the amount of intuition that goes into their reading. Some oracles give cut and dried answers that need no interpretation; others present complicated symbolic patterns that require a great deal of intuitive skill to interpret. The Coelbren falls somewhere in the middle range between these extremes. Its meanings are by no means whatever you want them to be—if you ask about whether something is going to continue going the way it's currently going and you get the Coelbren letter E, for example, don't try to argue that around to saying "yes"—but some degree of intuition is useful in narrowing down the range of possible meanings into a specific answer.

The basic meanings of the Coelbren letter E, for example, are "motion checked, interrupted, or broken, an indirect, negative, or distorted condition." As you consider the letter in the reading, you'll often find that one of these meanings stands out more strongly to you than the others, and practice will teach you how far to trust that flicker of insight. The practice of daily divination, as discussed later in this chapter, is a very useful way to learn this.

What is divination?

Before we go on to the practical methods of Coelbren divination, though, it's worth considering a question that's too often neglected: what exactly is divination? The word comes from Latin and has the same root as "divinity," which offers a useful hint of its original meaning. *Divinatio* quite literally meant consulting the gods and goddesses to ask for their guidance, and devout Romans—like people in most ancient societies—believed that the deities they worshipped spoke to them through such apparently random phenomena as the flight of birds and the direction from which thunder boomed on a stormy day. Many devout Christians interpret events in their lives in the same way, and with perfect logic: if God governs all things, why shouldn't His people pay close attention to His actions in the world of nature?

While there are still plenty of people who pay attention to natural signs in this way, the most popular kinds of divination these days are the kind that's called *sortilege*. This word stands for any divination method where the practitioner draws one or more symbols from a fixed set and interprets them. The runes and the Ogham letters are examples of symbol-sets that can be used for sortilege; so, of course, are tarot cards and a great many other modern oracles; and so, finally, are the letters of the Coelbren of the Bards.

One of the reasons many modern people look askance at any kind of divination, whether it uses sortilege, natural omens, or something else, is the common belief that purely random events like the flight of birds or the particular Coelbren letter that drops out of a bag into a diviner's hand can't possibly communicate any meaning worth knowing. Thus it may be helpful to talk a little about why divination can actually work. There are plenty of theories that try to explain this; with very few exceptions, all of them fall into one of three categories.

Nonrandomness explanations. The seemingly commonsense concept of "random chance" is a surprisingly difficult one to justify. Many scientists have argued that everything that happens in the world is the result of chains of cause and effect so strict that, given enough data and data-processing capacity, it would be possible to predict the future of the entire universe from the conditions of matter, energy, and motion in existence right now. Parallel to this scientific perspective is the very common religious belief that everything that happens in the world is subject to divine providence.

A similar approach through nonrandomness is the theory of synchronicity, which was developed in the early twentieth century by psychologist Carl Jung and quantum physicist Wolfgang Pauli.[47] Jung had noticed throughout his career as a therapist that his patient's lives, and also his own, were full of what he called "meaningful coincidences"— apparently chance events that had obvious personal meaning in their context. Pauli pointed out that quantum theory challenged ordinary notions of cause and effect, by showing that events could influence one another even when they weren't connected in space and time. Combining these insights, the two men proposed that everything in the universe is linked by a web of mutual influences that the human mind does not normally perceive, but can catch through certain means—divination among them.

Different as these theories are, they all deny that anything in the cosmos is actually random. According to both Jung and Pauli, there is always an underlying reason and order to events, even when human beings are unable to figure out what that is. To this way of seeing things, the diviner simply adds one detail: because all things follow an

---

[47] Jung 1960.

underlying reason and order, and all things are connected, it's possible to interpret the events of the present to foresee some of the possibilities of the future, or to sense hidden things by their reflections in visible things. The "random" fall of Coelbren letters, or any other symbol set, thus becomes a sample of the state of the cosmos, which the diviner can learn to read.

Diviner-centered explanations. Another possibility that has been much discussed is the suggestion that the mind of the person who practices divination, rather than the divination tools themselves, provides the link to meaning that makes a divination make sense of the future or the unknown present. Back in the middle years of the twentieth century, research into the subject of divination focused on what was then called "extrasensory perception"—that is, the ability of the human mind to pick up information by some means other than the five ordinary senses. It was suggested at that time that the tools of divination simply provided a convenient focus for the mind of the diviner, which could somehow tap into hidden sources of information.

More recently, diviner-centered explanations of divination have more often focused on the phenomenon of intuition. Put simply, all of us know more about the world than we realize. We receive information about the world constantly through our senses whenever we are awake, and in some states of shallow sleep as well, but under normal circumstances we can only draw on a small fraction of that flood of data. A sufficiently general set of symbols combined in random patterns, like the inkblot pictures used by psychologists to tease out unspoken perceptions, can jolt us into a sudden awareness of some part of this hidden knowledge, and allow us to make use of it in our lives.

Game theory explanations. Game theory was developed by the mathematician and physicist John von Neumann in the middle of the twentieth century. Even though it involves a great deal of very complex math, it's become a hugely important tool for decision making in the years since then, because quite a few of its most important concepts can be popped loose from their mathematical moorings and used as successful guidelines for strategy.

One of the things that game theory proved is that where strategy is concerned, a touch of randomness is a very good thing. If your strategy is absolutely predictable, after all, the other side will soon learn to predict it, while including a random element in decision making makes it harder for anyone to guess what you will do and forestall you. In many tribal societies, for example, hunters use some kind of divination to help decide where they will hunt each day; from a game theory standpoint, this is an excellent move, because many game animals have evolved the ability to learn the habits of predators, and the random factor of divination keeps the hunters from establishing habits that their prey can recognize and evade.

The same principle applies in every department of life. Human beings fall into habits of action, but also of perception; half the ruts that keep people making the same mistakes over and over again are ways of thinking about some common situation that keep everyone involved from seeing the possibility of less unpleasant outcomes. This is where divination works its magic. In any situation, there are plenty of unrecognized aspects; drawing one or more symbols in some random manner and then asking yourself, "How does this symbol relate to the situation?" is an effective way of jolting the mind out of its ruts and learning to see things in different ways, so that old mistakes can be avoided and new possibilities explored.

Hidden patterns within apparent randomness, subtle perceptions on the part of the diviner, or the sudden jolt of new perspectives predicted by game theory: which of these is responsible for the benefits of divination? Nobody knows for sure. It may be any of them, or all of them—there's no reason to assume that divination works in only one way—and other factors may play a part as well. The point that matters, ultimately, is that divination quite routinely provides startling and valuable insights into the shape of the future and the questions of everyday life. Give it an honest trial, and you'll soon discover the truth of this for yourself.

Making a Coelbren set

In order to do this, of course, you'll need a set of Coelbrens that you can use for divination. That's not something you can expect to find on sale in many places! A few online suppliers do offer sets of stones marked with the Coelbren letters, and this is certainly an option for those who can afford it. Another option, though, is making a set for yourself.

What do you need to make a set of Coelbrens for divination? That depends very much on what materials you want to use and how simple or complex you want the result to be. You can certainly use the classic approach outlined above, harvesting, drying, splitting, and preparing branches of the wood of your choice. If you choose this route, you'll want to spend some time practicing with a knife on wood until you can make the Coelbren letters clear and readable. The ebillion you use for each letter should be short, no more than two or three inches long. It's helpful to write the letter on all four sides, and to put them close to one end rather than in the middle of the ebill.

Why near one end? This points out one of the main differences between the Coelbren and similar letter-oracles such as the runes. If you rotate a rune so that the top now points down and vice versa, you can still recognize the rune. If you rotate a Coelbren letter in the same way, you've got a different letter: A becomes W, Bi becomes Pi, Ci becomes Di, and so on all through the alphabet. When you're making a set of Coelbrens, in other words, you need to make sure that you can recognize at a glance which end is the top of the letter. For the same reason, where some other divination systems assign a different meaning to a symbol when it's reversed than when it's upright, the Coelbren doesn't work that way. This is why only one divinatory meaning was given to each of the Coelbren letters in the previous chapter, not an upright meaning and a reversed one.

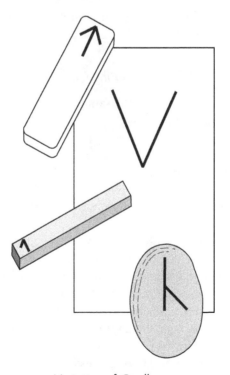

Varieties of Coelbren

The classic wooden ebill isn't the only way you can make a set of Coelbrens, of course. You can also use a wood burning pen, which can be bought at most hobby stores, to burn the letters onto short square wooden rods, which many hobby stores also carry. You can get small flat pieces of wood—anything from popsicle sticks on up will do—and use a wood burning pen, a permanent marker, or any other way of marking wood to put the letters on them. You can buy polymer clay at a hobby or craft store, make a set of Coelbrens out of that, and harden them in your oven. If you have the skill, you can carve the letters into pieces of wood or stone, or make a set out of clay and fire it in a kiln. Then there's the simplest way of all to make a set of Coelbrens: get twenty-four note cards or small pieces of paper and simply write the letters on them.

It's useful to have a small cloth bag or some other container in which to keep your Coelbren set, and many diviners like to spread a cloth on the table or other surface where they will be casting their readings. Some diviners, when casting a reading for someone else, prefer to have the other person draw the Coelbren letters for the reading, while others prefer to have no one else handle their Coelbren set. All of these are matters of personal choice, though, and you can do any, all, or none of these things as you prefer.

Divining with the Coelbren

No two diviners work in exactly the same way, and for that reason there are no hard and fast rules on how to cast readings with the Coelbren, or for that matter any other divinatory system. The suggestions given here are just that, suggestions. Feel free to explore them, experiment with them, and try other things that appeal to you. The important thing isn't to follow some approved set of procedures, it's to become comfortable with the Coelbren and the art of divination so that you can use it easily and get clear readings.

Familiarizing yourself with the letters is an important step, but since there are only twenty-four of them, this isn't hard. You can treat the Coelbren set as though it's a set of flash cards: draw one and see if you can remember its name, sound, and basic meaning, then repeat. Since the meaning of the letters relates so directly to the sound, pronouncing the letter name out loud can be helpful in this exercise.

Once you've familiarized yourself with the Coelbren letters and their basic meanings, you're ready to begin divining. The skill of divination, like most other skills, is best learned by regular practice, and the sooner you begin and the more readings you cast, the sooner you'll get past the awkward early phases of the learning curve. There are many different patterns in which you can lay out the letters for a reading; it's often easiest to start out with the simple patterns and work up from there, but you'll want to experiment to see whether this is true for you or not.

Many students of divination have found that one of the best ways to learn divination is to cast a reading every day, either early in the morning or late in the evening. The question to ask is "What do I most need to understand about the day ahead of me?" Use one of the simple reading patterns—the three rays of light reading given below on page 61–62 is a particularly good choice—and do your best to interpret the letters you draw. Write down the letters and your interpretation, and when the day is done, go back over your reading and see how well you did.

Very often, if you do this, you'll discover that the letters you drew actually predicted something very important about the day, but your interpretation didn't catch that aspect of their meaning. Don't be upset when this happens! You've just received corrective feedback, which will help you to read the letters more accurately the next time around. After a few months of daily readings, you'll have a solid personal grasp of what each of the Coelbren letters means to you, and your readings will improve steadily in accuracy and insight.

Some students have a great deal of trouble, especially at first, weaving together the cut and dried meanings of the letters into an interpretation that makes sense of the reading as a whole. One way to get past this difficulty is to think of interpreting a reading as a kind of storytelling. You are the main character in the story; the Coelbren letters you draw give you the incidents in the story, and those incidents happen in the order set out by the reading pattern. Tell the story as you imagine it and then, later on, compare the story you told with the events you were trying to predict or understand. You'll find that surprisingly often, your imagination will have tapped into the deeper sources of insight divination is meant to access.

In order to learn from your readings, of course, it's necessary to copy them down in some relatively permanent form. If divination by the Coelbren was actually practiced by Welsh bards in those distant times when a wooden ebill and a knife were easier to come by than paper and a pen, it's entirely possible that records of readings were made on ebillion in the time-honored fashion. In Iolo's time, paper and pens were a more likely medium. Nowadays, the Coelbren diviner can choose between a paper notebook and an electronic file on a laptop computer, tablet, or smartphone. Which option you pick is up to you—you can even keep your divination records on peithynen, if you really want to!—but it's important to record your readings, and to go back over them from time to time and see what you can learn from them.

With that in mind, we can proceed to the reading patterns.

The one letter reading

This is the simplest reading you can do with the Coelbren, but sometimes—when all you need is a straightforward hint as to the nature of the situation you're in—it's the most useful of them all. Ask a question along the lines of "What's going on here?" or "What do I need to understand about this situation?" In this and all other forms of Coelbren divination, the question you choose is of great importance, because everything in the reading will refer back to it. Take your time to make sure your question is actually the thing you most want to know!

Once you've stated your question, draw a single Coelbren. Its meaning will give you a concise answer to your question. Depending on the circumstances and your own skill with the Coelbren, you may then want to follow that reading up with a more detailed divination; alternatively, the Coelbren you draw may give you as much information as you wish.

Sample divination 1. Olwen is stuck in an ongoing conflict with a coworker who seems to relish the role of permanent adversary. Whatever she suggests, he inevitably criticizes, and not in any helpful fashion. Her attempts to discuss the matter with him have gone nowhere. One day, after a particularly difficult project meeting, she takes a few moments of solitude during her lunch break to consult the Coelbren. Her question is, "What do I need to know about this situation with my coworker?"

The Coelbren she draws is Ti, which means "Tension, drawing, or straining; stretching or drawing out; bringing to an end; confinement or termination."

Ti

Divination 1

Considering this, she realizes that it's telling her that the situation is approaching its end, and decides not to let her coworker get to her. Three days later she hears that the coworker has given notice, having decided to take a job in another city. Two weeks after that he is gone for good, and his replacement turns out to be much more pleasant to work with.

The three rays of light

Although a single Coelbren letter can sometimes provide as much information as you need, far more often you will want to use more than one. The three rays of light pattern is a good basic divination for general use. It's particularly recommended for the daily reading discussed above, but you'll find that it will give a clear overview of any situation and, if you phrase the question this way, cogent advice for what to do.

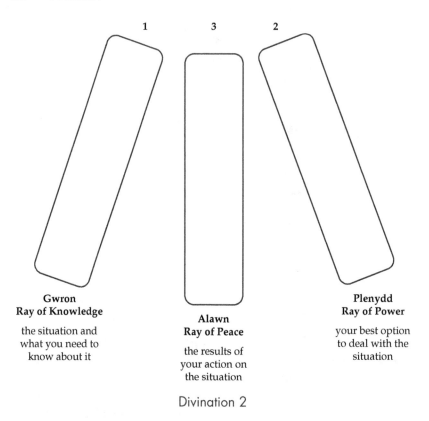

Gwron
Ray of Knowledge

the situation and
what you need to
know about it

Alawn
Ray of Peace

the results of
your action on
the situation

Plenydd
Ray of Power

your best option
to deal with the
situation

Divination 2

This reading pattern is based on the symbolism of the three rays of light, /|\, that Einigan the Giant saw at the creation of the world. Each of these rays has a name and a symbolic meaning. The left hand ray, /, is named Gwron (pronounced GOO-ron), which means "virtue"; it is the Ray of Knowledge. The right hand ray, \, is named Plenydd (pronounced PLEN-uth), which means "light"; it is the Ray of Power. The central ray, |, is named Alawn (pronounced ALL-awn), which means "harmony"; it is the Ray of Peace.

The three Coelbren letters are thus drawn and laid out in the order just given—left, right, and center. The first one represents the situation and what you need to know about it. The second represents you and the options you have available. The third represents the outcome of the situation or the results of your action.

Sample divination 2. Dylan, an aspiring musician in a folk-rock band, is casting his daily divination, and his question as usual is "What do I most need to understand about this day's events?" The Coelbren letters he draws are Lli, Si, and Ffi.

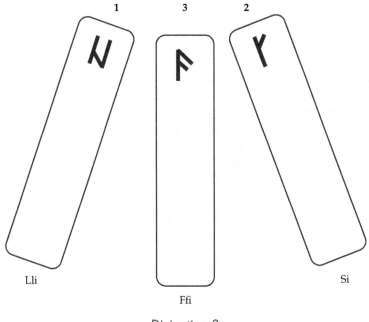

Divination 3

The First Ray is Lli. Its meanings are "Turbulence, confusion, and disruption; difficulty in proceeding; obstacles, solidity, movement requires effort." As the First Ray, it represents the situation he faces in the day before him. He knows from this that he's facing a day full of disruptions and complications, and it's going to require effort to get anything done at all.

The Second Ray is Si. Its meanings are "Inferiority, secrecy, privacy; a secret or private knowledge or indication; insinuation, indirect action." As the Second Ray, it represents his best option for dealing with the situation. He knows from this that he won't have any way to make the disruptions and complications stop, and his best bet is to keep his head down and his mouth shut, and try to avoid being drawn into the mess.

The Third Ray is Ffi. Its meanings are "Causation, impulsion, setting a thing or action in motion, the source or initial impetus of change or activity." As the Third Ray, it represents the results Dylan's action will have on the situation. He knows from this that if he follows the advice of the Second Ray, the result will be that some situation in his life that's been stuck in a holding pattern will be pushed into motion, and it also seems likely that the need to get things moving is the hidden driving force behind the rest of the reading.

Nothing out of the ordinary happens at Dylan's day job working at a restaurant. That evening, though, when he arrives at the rented space where his band practices, a screaming fight has already broken out between the lead guitarist and the keyboard player. Partly a clash of egos, partly a disagreement about the direction the band is headed in terms of style and repertoire, the conflict has been building for some time, absorbing energy and time that could have gone into practicing and playing gigs. In the past, Dylan has tried to mediate between them, but this time, remembering the advice of his daily divination, he says nothing and lets the fight play out. Finally the lead guitarist walks out and slams the door behind him. Dylan and the other members of the band sit down, talk it over, and settle the few remaining issues, before picking up their instruments and practicing with renewed enthusiasm.

The Cauldron of Annwn

In Welsh legend, the Cauldron of Annwn was the mysterious vessel from which souls were born and reborn. This reading pattern allows a glimpse at the whole trajectory of a situation from beginning to end.

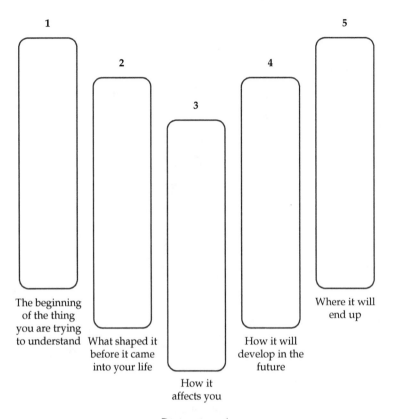

The beginning of the thing you are trying to understand

What shaped it before it came into your life

How it affects you

How it will develop in the future

Where it will end up

Divination 4

There are five letters in the Cauldron of Annwn reading, and they run from left to right as shown in the diagram. The first is the beginning of whatever you are asking about. The second is what shapes it before it comes into your life. The third is its effects on you. The fourth is where it is headed in the future, and the fifth is where it will end up.

Sample divination 3. Anwyl has been offered a transfer to a new department at the company where she works. The position she has been offered has better pay, but she is uncertain about whether she would be better off taking the offer or staying in her current job. The Coelbren letters she draws are Mi, Chi, Fi, E, and Ti.

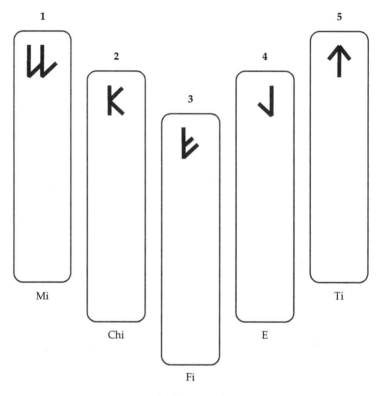

Divination 5

Mi means "Comprehending, embracing, or surrounding; enclosure or capacity, inclusion within something; large or complex." In the first position of this reading pattern, it cautions Anwyl that there is much more going on here than she realizes. Behind the creation of the new department and the transfer she's been offered stands some larger and more complex situation.

Chi means "Conflict, opposition, obstacle; mutual interference between two or more contending forces or things." In the second position of this reading pattern, it tells her that some kind of conflict has been going on behind the scenes, and suggests that this might be the hidden context indicated by the first letter.

Fi means "Protection, limitation, discipline, establishment or maintenance of order; response unfavorable to an external cause or stimulus."

In the third position of this reading pattern, it suggests to Anwyl that she should be wary of the proposed transfer and might well be better off remaining where she is.

E means "Motion checked, interrupted, or broken, an indirect, negative, or distorted condition." In the fourth position of this reading pattern, it warns her that if she accepts the transfer, nothing is going to go the way she expects, and a great many difficulties and complications can be expected.

Ti means "Tension, drawing, or straining; stretching or drawing out; bringing to an end; confinement or termination." In the last position of this reading pattern, it predicts that the new department and the positions associated with it may not last long.

After reflecting on the reading and gathering as much information as she can, Anwyl turns down the transfer and stays in her current job. Six months later, she is glad she did so, as the new department is abruptly shut down, and many of its employees are laid off. Two weeks later, word comes back from corporate headquarters that the vice-president who pushed the creation of the new department has been forced out, and Anwyl hears by way of the office grapevine later on that two other vice-presidents deliberately sabotaged the new department in order to get rid of a rival.

Gwydion and the pigs

In the *Mabinogion*, the greatest of the cycles of Welsh legend, the enchanter Gwydion steals the first pigs in Wales from Pryderi, King of Dyfed, and drives them north through Wales to his own province of Gwynedd. This theft provided the push that set in motion the events of the Fourth Branch of the *Mabinogion*. In this reading, the letter that represents Gwydion is a specific change or event the diviner is considering, and the pigs are the consequences that unfold from that change or event. The Gwydion and the pigs spread is a useful reading pattern whenever you need to figure out what results will follow from a decision you're considering or an event you think might happen.

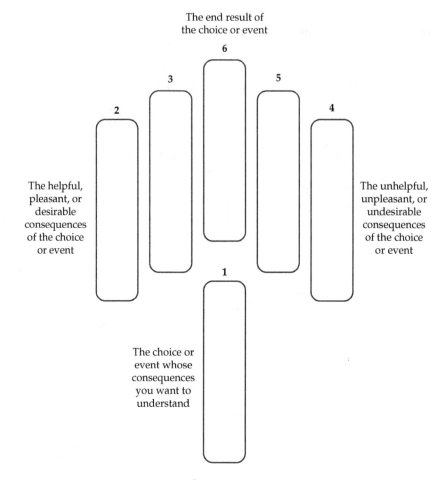

The end result of
the choice or event

6

3

5

2

4

The helpful,
pleasant, or
desirable
consequences
of the choice
or event

The unhelpful,
unpleasant, or
undesirable
consequences
of the choice
or event

1

The choice or
event whose
consequences
you want to
understand

Divination 6

There are six letters in the Gwydion and the pigs reading. The first, representing Gwydion, is the event or decision that sets things into motion. The second and third—the first two pigs—are the helpful, pleasant, or comforting consequences of the event or decision; the second arrives in the near future, the third later on. The fourth and fifth—the next two pigs—are the unwelcome, unpleasant, or challenging consequences of the event or decision; the fourth arrives in the near future, the fifth later on. The sixth, the last pig, is the end result of the event or decision, and sums up the consequences in itself.

Sample divination 4. Llewellyn is considering proposing to his girl-friend Sioned, with whom he's been living for the last two years. The Coelbren letters he draws are A, Li, Hi, Mi, Ddi, I.

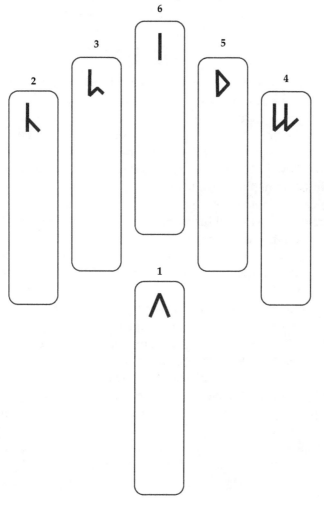

Divination 7

A means "proceeding forward; continuation in the same state or condition, whether of motion, action, or rest." As the first letter in this reading pattern, Gwydion's card, it represents the decision that sets the reading in motion, and it points out to Llewellyn that deciding to propose is simply the next logical step in his relationship with Sioned, a step toward which they have both been moving for some time.

Li means "Flow, softness, smoothness, lightness, open space, solution or evanescence, movement without effort, as gliding." As the second letter in this reading pattern, it represents positive consequences in the near term, and suggests to him that proceeding from living together to marriage will be easy for the two of them.

Hi means "Generation, abundance, fertility, nurturance and support, response favorable to an external cause or stimulus." As the third letter in this reading pattern, it represents positive consequences in the longer term, and predicts that marriage with Sioned will in fact be a positive and nurturing experience. It also reminds Llewellyn that children are likely to follow in due time, and he spends some time thinking about what kind of father he wants to be.

Mi means "Comprehending, embracing, or surrounding; enclosure or capacity, inclusion within something; large or complex." As the fourth letter in this reading pattern, it represents challenging or unwelcome consequences in the short term, and cautions Llewellyn that getting married will involve a good many complexities—more, perhaps, than he expects.

Ddi means "Realm, extent, or field of action; territory; boundary, surface, or interface marking the limit of a given force or influence." As the fifth letter in this reading pattern, it represents challenging or unwelcome consequences in the longer term, and reminds him that choosing to get married involves accepting certain definite limits on his future actions.

I, finally, means "The movement of a thing to its proper place, being or becoming a part of a whole, approach, applicability, subordination." As the last letter in this reading pattern, it sums up the consequences of the original action. Llewellyn ponders it, and realizes that proposing to Sioned feels to him exactly like moving into his proper place, and becoming part of a whole defined by the two of them and the family they will raise.

Two nights later, as they finish dinner at a favorite restaurant, he gathers up his courage and asks the question. Three months later, after an exhausting series of interactions with members of both families who seem to go out of their way to be difficult, the wedding takes place. A year later, as he and Sioned settle into a new home, Llewellyn looks back over the reading in the notebook and nods, sure that he has made the right choice.

The Celtic cross

This classic tarot reading pattern works equally well with the Coelbren. It is well suited whenever you want an overall view of your current situation in life, or that of another person for whom you are doing the reading. There are ten letters in the reading, as shown below.

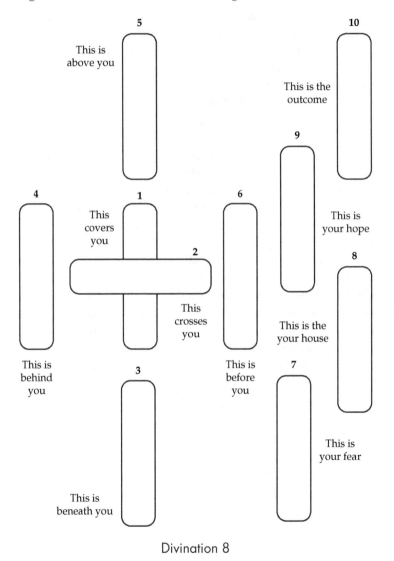

Divination 8

The first letter represents the factor that helps and protects you, and furthers your goals. The words traditionally said while laying down this letter are "This covers you."

The second letter represents the factor that opposes and challenges you, and stands in the way of your goals. The words here are "This crosses you."

The third letter represents the factor that forms the foundation or basis of the situation. The words are "This is beneath you."

The fourth letter represents something in the past, which you are moving out of. The words are "This is behind you."

The fifth letter represents something you may be able to achieve in the situation. The words are "This is above you."

The sixth letter represents something in the future, toward which you are moving. The words are "This is before you."

The seventh letter represents something that frightens or upsets you. The words here are "This is your fear."

The eighth letter represents the influence of your friends and family, and other people who affect you. The words are "This is your house."

The ninth letter represents your hopes and dreams in the situation. The words are "This is your hope."

The tenth letter represents the final outcome of the situation, and the words are, "This is the outcome."

Sample divination 5. Branwen, a university student, has asked Rhiannon, a fellow student and Coelbren diviner, to cast a reading for her about her life in general. After a cup of tea and a quarter hour of pleasant conversation, Rhiannon gets out her Coelbren set and casts the reading. The letters she draws are Bi, W, Ddi, I, Hi, Lli, Ri, Mi, O, Pi.

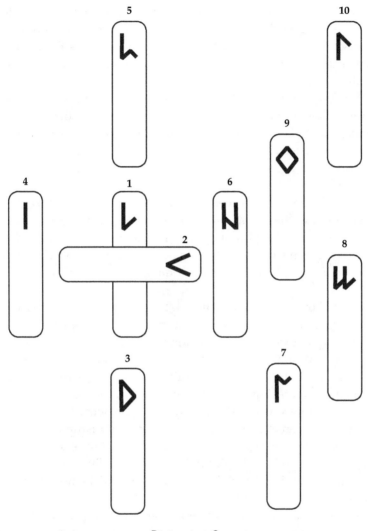

Divination 9

"This covers you," Rhiannon says, setting down Bi. The letter means "The being of any thing in a quiescent state, a condition or state of being, mere existence, perception," and as the first letter in this reading pattern, it means that Branwen is in a good place in her life right now and has much to gain by staying right where she is.

"This crosses you," says Rhiannon, and sets down W. The letter means "Sorting or distributing things into different classes or categories, discrimination, divergence, choosing." This shows Rhiannon that others may be trying to push Branwen into making some kind of decision she isn't ready to make.

"This is beneath you." Rhiannon sets down Ddi; this letter means "Realm, extent, or field of action; territory; boundary, surface, or interface marking the limit of a given force or influence." This tells her that Branwen has based her success in life so far on being careful to focus her efforts on things she knows she can do well, and accepting the limits this involves.

"This is behind you." Rhiannon sets down I; this letter means "The movement of a thing to its proper place, being or becoming a part of a whole, approach, applicability, subordination." This reveals that the process of getting herself into an appropriate situation and finding her niche in the world has occupied much of Branwen's efforts up to this time.

"This is above you," says Rhiannon. The next letter is Hi, which means "Generation, abundance, fertility, nurturance and support, response favorable to an external cause or stimulus." This might be simply an indication that Branwen might be able to maintain her nurturing and supportive niche, but Rhiannon's intuition tells her otherwise: Branwen is thinking about taking on a nurturing and supporting role for others.

"This is before you," Rhiannon says next. The letter for this position is Lli, which means "Turbulence, confusion, and disruption; difficulty in proceeding; obstacles, solidity, movement requires effort." This is a warning that the relatively placid life Branwen is living right now will not be able to continue much longer. Some form of disruption waits for her in the future.

"This is your fear," says Rhiannon, and sets down Ri. This letter means "Force, prevalence, or superiority; an action performed by main strength; excess, tearing or breaking, causing damage." This shows that what Branwen fears most about her present situation is the possibility that her life will be disrupted by forces out of her control.

"This is your house," says Rhiannon, and sets down Mi. This letter means "Comprehending, embracing, or surrounding; enclosure or capacity, inclusion within something; large or complex." It shows Rhiannon that a great many people are putting pressure on Branwen right now, pushing in many different directions, and she feels surrounded and overwhelmed.

"This is your hope." Rhiannon sets down O. This letter means "Movement outward or away from, departure, rejection or projection, casting or putting forth." All at once Rhiannon realizes the implication: Branwen is afraid of being forced out of her comfortable existence, but she's also tired of it, and ready to leave it if she can do so on her own terms.

"This is the outcome," Rhiannon says finally, and sets down Pi. This letter means "Pushing, penetrating, springing or putting forth; a protrusion or prominence, sharpness, convexity." The outcome, Rhiannon sees, is that it's time for Branwen to leave her current situation and do something else with her life. This won't be easy, and it will require her to make a clean break with many things—and quite possibly some people—that belong to the life she's about to leave behind. If she does so, though, she will have a real chance of fulfilling her dreams.

Rhiannon explains all this to Branwen, who has had Coelbren readings before and so isn't surprised to find her life spread out in front of her this way. She explains to Rhiannon that she's very comfortable and happy at university, but graduation is not too many months off and she has to make plans for what to do thereafter. Her family has been pressing her to pursue some kind of well-paying corporate job, but the job market is very tough, and the thought of spending the next thirty or forty years of her life in the corporate world makes her blood run cold. She would like, she thinks, to proceed to graduate school and try for an academic career, but she's worried about how her family will take the news, and also whether she can handle the more challenging work she'll face in graduate school.

Two pots of tea and a very long conversation later, Branwen has decided to follow her dreams. Rhiannon casts another reading for her six weeks later to help her decide which of half a dozen graduate programs to pursue, and three months after that she gets an excited phone call from Branwen, who's just been accepted into graduate school.

CHAPTER FIVE

Coelbren symbolism

ᚱᚢᚲᚨᚦᚦᛁᚲᛘᚮᚱ

> A symbol is a form that is understood, and being understood, shows at sight that which really exists which would require many letters, or much of vocal song, or speech and oration, before it could be properly understood.
>
> —*Barddas*[48]

Divination is the simplest use of the Coelbren, other than ordinary writing, and the use that most people take up first, just as most people who study the runes, the Ogham, or the tarot think of them primarily as methods for divination. Like these and other sets of oracular symbols, however, the Coelbren has a much broader range of applications for those who want to pursue them. It can be a potent tool for many kinds of inner work.

What is a symbol? Philosophers have been wrestling with that question for a very long time, but for our present purposes we can settle on a simple answer: a symbol is something that means something. More precisely, it's a thing you can experience with the five ordinary senses, but stands for an entire constellation of meanings.

---

[48] Williams ab Ithel 2004, p. 93.

A letter can be seen with your eyes and also, if it's cut into a piece of wood, felt with your fingertips, but it means much more than the senses themselves convey. If it belongs to a sacred alphabet such as the Coelbren, it means much more than the sound it expresses or the words that it forms.

Writing systems have been used for symbolic purposes since the beginning of history. Egyptian priests and priestesses used their language's hieroglyphic writing as a rich source of images, as Chinese Taoists do today with the equally intricate characters of written Chinese. In ancient Greece, a sequence of letters called the *Ephesia grammata*, "writing of Ephesus," was believed to have magic powers. To this day, the English word "spell" means both the process of writing a word correctly and a magic charm. The Coelbren, too, can be used for symbolic purposes. We'll look at several of the options in this chapter.

The meaning of names

One standard way to use alphabets as a source of symbolic insight is to apply them as symbols to decode the meanings of names and words of power. This may seem arbitrary at first, until you remember that many names and words of power were deliberately constructed to have meanings that are meant to be decoded in this way. One good example is OIW, the cryptic name of the Divine that conceals the Secret of the Bards of the Isle of Britain. As far as the evidence suggests, Iolo Morganwg created this name, and it makes sense to assume that he did it with an eye toward the meanings of the Coelbren letters that spell it. We can take it a letter at a time.

◇ The letter O stands for outward movement, sending something out or away, departure, projection, putting something forth. As part of a divine name it immediately suggests the idea of the creation of the world and of the individual soul.

❘ The letter I has the opposite meaning, and stands for the movement of a thing into its proper place, approach, indrawing, being or becoming part of a unity. As part of a divine name it immediately suggests the idea of redemption, the return of the soul to its proper place after its wanderings.

V   The letter W resolves the tension between these two words. It stands for sorting or distributing things into their proper categories, separation, and choosing. As part of a divine name it immediately suggests the idea of judgment, of a final sorting out where everything goes to its proper place.

The divine name OIW thus sums up the concept of God that was familiar to Iolo and his students: the Creator of the universe who calls His children to return to Him, and who will eventually judge the world. While there is considerably more hidden in the name OIW than this, Iolo chose the name well, so that it would communicate to the attentive student something of the spiritual background of his bardic teaching.

According to *Barddas*, the name OIW was one of the first three words of the original Welsh language.[49] The other two were Sulw, the ancient name of the sun, and Byw, which means both "world" and "life" in Welsh. Let's examine these two words through their symbolism.

ᚠ   The letter Si represents a secret, something hidden or private, something that cannot be known by those outside the circle of secrecy. It can also stand for indirect action. In Iolo's time, the source of the sun's light and heat was a complete mystery to scientists.

Y   The letter U represents wholeness, completeness, and unity, and can mean the background or context in which everything else takes place. In Iolo's time as in ours, most people knew that the sun was the pivot around which the whole solar system turned, and that its light and heat made life possible on Earth.

ᚲ   The letter Li represents flow, lightness, open space, and movement without effort. It well represents the effortless outward flow of the sun's rays throughout the vast open space of the solar system.

V   Yet the sun does not shine on every part of Earth evenly, or all the time. There is a process of distribution and divergence by which the sun's light spreads unequally over the world, flooding the tropics with heat and light while sending only a pale light to

---

[49] Williams ab Ithel 2004, p. 71.

the poles, and shining brightly at noontide while being completely hidden at midnight. This is clearly represented by the letter W, as already discussed.

The word Byw can be interpreted in a similar way:

L   The letter Bi stands for existence itself, the condition or state of being, and also the power of perception that allows us to experience what is. The traditional approach of sound symbolism fits well here—think of the English word "Be!" Life is existence; to be alive is to exist, and to perceive other things that exist.

Y   The letter Y stands for balance or suspension, impartiality, neutrality, a situation where all the various factors are taken into account but a decision has not yet been made one way or the other. As *Barddas* teaches,[50] human beings are poised midway between good and evil, free to choose one or the other at every moment.

V   The letter W, finally, once again stands for sorting or distribution, choosing, and judgment. This reminds us that our choices matter, and that our position as human beings balanced between good and evil is meant to allow us to choose good and thus prepare ourselves to rise up out of Abred, the world of incarnate existence, to Gwynfydd, the luminous life of spiritual existence.

This same kind of analysis can be applied to other words and names. Participants in the modern Druid Revival will find that it casts a fascinating light onto the names of the Druid gods and goddesses, on the names of people and places in the *Mabinogion* and other storehouses of old Welsh legend, and on the Welsh versions of the names of figures in the Arthurian legends. As far as anyone knows, the Coelbren of the Bards did not yet exist when these names were originally formulated, and it's a fascinating question why they should yield up relevant meanings when interpreted through the symbolism of the Coelbren—as in fact they do.

---

[50] Williams ab Ithel 2004, p. 177.

The colors of the Coelbren

Another element of letter symbolism used in many of the world's mystical and magical traditions is the assignment of a color to each letter. These assignments are always somewhat arbitrary, but as will be shown in the next two chapters, they have considerable practical usefulness. The colors I have found best suited to the Coelbren in practice are these:

A – sky blue	Hi – turquoise (blue-green)
E – dull white	Li – grass green
I – light red	Mi – chartreuse (yellow-green)
O – ultramarine	Ni – golden yellow
W – forest green	Pi – amber (yellow-orange)
Y – light gray	Ri – orange
U – black	Si – vermilion (red-orange)
Bi – cerise (violet red)	Ti – scarlet
Ci – violet	Ddi – light bluish purple
Di – purple	Lli – moss green
Ffi – indigo (blue-purple)	Fi – rust red
Gi – royal blue	Chi – dark brown

Some people have an easy time imagining these colors, while this is more difficult for others. If you belong to the latter category, it helps to start by becoming more familiar with the colors themselves. Most good sets of colored pencils include all the colors listed above, and it can be helpful to write out the full alphabet in colored pencil, writing each letter in its proper color, so that you get used to what the color looks like. The practice of color breathing, which is discussed in the next chapter, is also an effective way to learn how to imagine colors clearly.

The gematria of the Coelbren

A further dimension of Coelbren symbolism unfolds from the ancient custom of using letters to indicate numbers. Scholars nowadays call this by the tongue-twisting word isopsephy, but in Western esoteric circles it has long gone by the Hebrew label *gematria*.

Each word, according to gematria, has a hidden numerical meaning alongside its outward, literal meaning. This meaning is found by
adding up the numerical values of the letters that form the word. The
theory of gematria is that words that add up to the same number share
a secret meaning, and so one word that adds up to a given number
can be interpreted by other words that add up to the same number.
Hebrew assigns a number to each letter of its alphabet, and so gematria
is an important element of Jewish symbolism. One classic example in
Hebrew gematria unfolds from the most sacred of the divine names in
Jewish tradition, יהוה or YHVH, which adds to 26. The word אחד, achad,
"unity," adds to 13, and so does the word אהבה, ahevah, "love." To the
Jewish mystic, since 13 + 13 = 26, love plus unity give us our clearest
insight into the nature of the Divine.

An equally rich tradition of gematria uses the Greek alphabet, which
also assigns a number to each letter. Ancient Greek Pagan tradition
made much use of gematria. The New Testament, which was originally
written in Greek, is also full of gematria, and so are the writings of the
Gnostics, whose mystical understanding of Christian theology played
an important role in many underground currents of Western spirituality. One example out of many is the word τεμενος, temenos, the sacred
enclosure around an ancient Greek temple. It adds up to 670, which is
the same number as 'ο κοσμος, ho Kosmos, the universe. It was a common theme in ancient religion all around the world to see the temple
and its enclosure as a reflection of the universe, and the universe as a
temple in which the gods are always present; Greek gematria expressed
that insight with the precision of mathematics.

The Coelbren also has its gematria, though it is partly concealed
in the pages of *Barddas* and has to be pieced together on the basis of
clues Iolo and John Williams ab Ithel were careful not to make too obvious. Most of the clues can be found on two pages tucked away near
the end of the first section of *Barddas*.[51] There the letters A, E, I, and O
are assigned to the numbers 1, 2, 3, and 4 respectively. After that, the
discussion turns into a complete jumble, in which the same letters are
assigned to different numbers and vice versa. One of the few consistent
details in the mess that follows is that Di is pretty clearly meant to be
the number 10.

---

[51] Williams ab Ithel 2004, pp. 97 and 111.

The basic rule of gematria in all other systems that use it, however, is that the letters are assigned numbers in their normal alphabetical order. The consistent assignment of AEIO to the first four digits shows that the standard Coelbren order, with vowels first, is intended here. Do that, furthermore, and Di falls into the right place as 10. With that in mind, we can assign the Coelbren letters to their proper numbers in a straightforward manner:

A – 1	Di – 10	Si – 100
E – 2	Ffi – 20	Ti – 200
I – 3	Gi – 30	Ddi – 300
O – 4	Hi – 40	Lli – 400
W – 5	Li – 50	Fi – 500
Y – 6	Mi – 60	Chi – 600
U – 7	Ni – 70	
Bi – 8	Pi – 80	
Ci – 9	Ri – 90	

Numbers above 600 may have been assigned some of the letters used only by grammarians, but the evidence available to me does not allow the details to be worked out yet. Fortunately, the gematria of the twenty-four-letter Coelbren as shown above opens the doors to intriguing discoveries all by itself.

We can begin with the same three primal words explored earlier in this chapter: OIW, the concealed name of the Divine; Sulw, the name of the sun; and Byw, the word for life. O + I + W is 4 + 3 + 5 = 12, the traditional number of wholeness and completion—there are twelve signs in the zodiac, twelve months in the year, twelve apostles, and so on. B + Y + W is 8 + 6 + 5 = 19, and 19 is a traditional number of life—in fact, in Hebrew gematria it is the number value of the name חוה, Eve, which means "life" in Hebrew.

Sulw is more complex. S + U + L + W is 100 + 7 + 50 + 6 = 163, a prime number with no obvious role in traditional number symbolism. In Hebrew gematria it is the number of the word נוקבה, "woman," and of course it is one of the distinctive features of the Celtic traditions that they see the sun as female, rather than male. Double that number to 326, however, and you have the most important number in the Christian Cabala, the number of יהשוה, the name of Jesus. Since Iolo and most of his students were Christians of various kinds, some relatively orthodox and some (like Iolo himself) much less so, it's not surprising to find a reference to Christian tradition here—nor to find Sulw the sun represented as a partial emblem of the central Christian divinity, and thus one-half the numerical value.

A much broader field of symbolism is opened up by applying Coelbren gematria to other terms used in *Barddas*, and to important sources of Welsh tradition such as the *Mabinogion*. It is interesting, to use no stronger term, that Awen—the divine spirit of inspiration in Iolo's writings, and in Welsh lore generally—adds to the same number, 78, as the Hebrew word Mezla, the divine creative influence that descends through the Tree of Life. It's equally interesting to note that Coelbren gematria supports the suggestion by some Welsh scholars that Pryderi, the king of south Wales who plays an important role all through the Four Branches of the *Mabinogion*, was originally the same figure as Peredur, the hero of the Welsh version of the Grail legend. The two names have the same consonants, which helped spark the suggestion, but they also add up via Coelbren gematria to the same number, 281.

A great deal more can be done with the gematria of the Coelbren. I discovered the key to the number values of the Coelbren only a short time ago, and have already turned up fascinating things woven into the text of *Barddas* and other old Welsh documents such as the *Mabinogion*. Since nothing seems to have been done with this dimension of the Coelbren since John William ab Ithel's time, there may be secrets hidden away in Iolo's works that have been untouched for a century and a half, awaiting the keen eyes of students who have the tools to decipher them. With this in mind, Appendix 4 of this book includes a list of some important names and words from *Barddas* and the *Mabinogion*, with Coelbren gematria values included.

CHAPTER SIX

Coelbren meditation

Λレく✓>ΙΚΓΟΓ

> After the discovery of the knowledge of letters it was that
> every understanding, and consideration, and every meditation
> of awen were committed to the memorial of letters.
>
> —*Barddas*[52]

Most people these days tend to think of meditation as something mysterious and Oriental, and have no idea that the Western world has any meditation systems of its own. The irony is that in Iolo Morganwg's time, meditation was still a fairly common practice in Britain and elsewhere in the Western world; most people knew at least a little about it, and an extensive though mostly forgotten literature on meditation—nearly all of it phrased in terms of Christian spirituality—could be studied by anybody who had an interest in the subject.[53] Whether or not the students of Iolo's Bardic mysteries practiced some form of it is a question not yet settled, but it's certainly possible that they did.

---

[52] Williams ab Ithel 2004, p. 27.
[53] One of the few examples still in print is *Mystical Meditations on the Collects* by Dion Fortune, which is very much in the style of the older literature. See Fortune 1989.

There's nothing particularly unusual or exotic about meditation. It's simply what happens when we direct our mind to one subject and keep it there, instead of letting it jump from one topic to another like an enthusiastic squirrel. The English word "meditation," in fact, comes from a Latin word meaning "thinking," and the Welsh word for meditation, *myfyrdod*, has a similar origin—it's related to words such as *myfyrfa*, "study" (in the sense of a room where studying takes place), and *myfyriwr*, "student." The only thing that sets meditation apart from ordinary concentrated thinking is that certain useful habits have been developed over the years to help keep the mind focused and prevent physical and emotional tensions from getting in the way.

Meditation as it was practiced in Iolo's time usually focused either on verses from the Bible on the one hand, or short texts meant to improve the mind on the other. Booksellers in eighteenth- and nineteenth-century Britain carried entire books full of such texts, which usually had the word "meditation" somewhere in the title. That sort of textual meditation is still very much an option, of course,[54] but it's also possible to use other kinds of themes for meditation. Among the things that work well with the Western style of meditation are images that are easy to picture in the mind's eye, and have interesting patterns of meaning connected to them: the Coelbren, for example.

Preliminaries for meditation

For all of the meditation exercises in this chapter you'll need a place that's quiet and not too brightly lit. It should be private—a room with a door you can shut is best, though if you can't arrange that, a quiet corner and a little forbearance on the part of your housemates will do the job. You'll need a chair with a straight back and a seat at a height that allows you to rest your feet flat on the floor while keeping your thighs level with the ground. You'll need a clock or watch, placed so that you can see it easily without moving your head. You'll also need a journal to keep track of your meditations and the results you get. The journal in which you write down your Coelbren divinations can be used for this

---

[54] Large sections of *Barddas* seem to be designed to be used for this purpose, particularly the philosophical, theological, and symbolic triads in the second and third parts of the book.

as well, especially if you're doing a daily Coelbren reading as recommended in Chapter Three.

Only you can decide how often to practice meditation. Many people find that practicing meditation every day, preferably first thing in the morning, brings the best results. You may or may not be able to make time for this in your schedule, though, and if once a week is what you can do, that's what you can do. The calming and centering benefits of regular meditation are such that you may find yourself making room in your schedule for it!

The posture for Western meditation is much simpler, and more comfortable for most people, than the standard Asian postures. Sit on the chair with your feet and knees together or parallel, whichever is most comfortable for you. Your back should be straight but not stiff, your hands resting on your thighs, and your head rising as though a string fastened to the crown of your skull pulled it gently upwards. Your eyes may be open or closed as you prefer; if they're open, they should look ahead of you but not focus on anything in particular. Once you've gotten settled into the posture, you can proceed to the first of the preliminary exercises.

The key to meditation is learning to enter a state of relaxed concentration. The word "relaxed" needs to be kept in mind here. Too often, what "concentration" suggests to modern people is a kind of inner struggle: teeth clenched, eyes narrowed, the whole body taut with useless tension. This is the opposite of the state you need to reach. The exercises below will help you get to that state of relaxed but poised focus that will allow meditation to happen.

Preliminary exercise 1. Put yourself in the meditation position, and then spend ten minutes or so just being aware of your physical body. Start at the soles of your feet, your contact point with the earth, and work your way slowly upward to the crown of your head. Take your time, and notice any tensions you feel. Don't try to force yourself to relax; simply be aware of each point of tension. Over time this simple act of awareness will dissolve your body's habitual tensions by making them conscious, and bringing up the rigid patterns of thought and emotion that form their foundations. Like so much in meditation, though, this process has to unfold at its own pace.

While you're doing this exercise, let your body become as still as possible. You may find yourself wanting to fidget and shift, but resist the temptation. Whenever your body starts itching, cramping, or reacting against stillness in some other way, simply be aware of it, without responding to it. These reactions often become very intrusive during the first month or so of meditation practice, but bear with them. They show you that you're getting past the levels of ordinary awareness. The discomforts you're feeling are actually present in your body all the time; you've simply learned not to notice them. Now that you can perceive them again, you can relax into them and let them go.

Preliminary exercise 2. Do the first exercise for ten minutes daily for a week or so, until the posture starts to feel comfortable and balanced. After that, it's time to bring in the next part of meditation, which is breathing: specifically, a style of breathing that is called the "fourfold breath" in Western spiritual traditions. Start this phase of the practice by taking your meditation position and going through the first exercise quickly, as a way of "checking in" with your physical body and settling into a comfortable and stable position. Then turn your attention to your breath. Draw in a deep breath, and expel it slowly and steadily, until your lungs are completely empty.

When every last puff of air is out of your lungs, hold the breath out while counting slowly and steadily from one to four. Then breathe in through your nose, smoothly and evenly, counting from one to four. Hold your breath in, counting from one to four; it's important to hold the breath in by keeping the chest and belly expanded, not by shutting your throat, which can hurt your lungs. Breathe out through your nose, smoothly and evenly, again counting from one to four. Continue breathing at the same slow steady rhythm, counting in the same way, for ten minutes.

While you're breathing, your thoughts will likely try to stray onto some other topic. Don't let them. Keep your attention on the rhythm of the breathing, the feeling of the air moving into and out of your lungs. Whenever you notice that you're thinking about something else, bring your attention gently back to your breathing. If your thoughts slip away again, bring them back again. With practice, you'll find it increasingly easy to keep your mind centered on the simple process of breathing.

As that happens, the first of the positive effects of meditation will start to show themselves. Most people find that they become calmer and more focused after a session of meditation, even if all that's involved is this kind of steady rhythmic breathing. You may also find that your body is less tense, and some people even find that they need less sleep when they meditate every day.

Color breathing

While you're working with the second preliminary exercise, you may want to add the art of color breathing to your practices. This is a way of combining breath and imagination to work with consciousness. It requires a certain amount of practice imagining colors, and a specific set of colors that have symbolic meanings. The colors assigned to the Coelbren in the previous chapter provide the second of these requirements, and the first can be gained by the exercise with colored pencils included there, or in any other way that appeals to you.

The method of color breathing is extremely simple. When you have finished the brief period of relaxation and begin concentrating on your breathing, imagine that you are in an infinite ocean of colored light. Above you, below you, and to all sides, there is nothing but light of whatever color you have chosen. As you breathe in, imagine that colored light flows in through your nostrils along with the air, filling your entire body. As you hold your breath in, imagine the colored light present all through your body. As you breathe out, imagine the colored light flowing back out of your body until you are completely emptied of it. As you hold your breath out, imagine the colored light surrounding your body again. Repeat this with each cycle of the fourfold breath you perform.

The color you use for color breathing is up to you. In the Coelbren meditations that follow, you will find it most effective to use the color assigned to the letter—sky blue with A, dull white with E, and so on. While you're learning color breathing, on the other hand, feel free to experiment with a range of colors, and see what effects they have on you.

Coelbren meditation

Do the second preliminary exercise, with or without color breathing, for ten minutes daily for a week or two, until you feel that your mind has started to become clearer while you practice the fourfold breath. At this point it's time to bring in the third dimension of meditation practice, the dimension of the mind. The best way to do this is to proceed to Coelbren meditation itself.

Start by selecting what the traditional meditation literature calls a theme—that is, an idea or image you want to understand better. To begin with, the letters of the Coelbren alphabet are the most suitable theme for you to work with. Later on, you can explore combinations of the letters, especially as found in the important names and words of *Barddas* and other sources of ancient bardic lore, and you can also go on to a wide range of other themes. Meditation is a key that opens many doors.

Sit down in the meditation posture, and spend a minute or two going through the first preliminary exercises, being aware of your body and its tensions. Then begin the fourfold breath, and continue it for five minutes by the clock, using the color breathing method described above with the color assigned to the letter you've chosen as your theme. During these first steps, don't think about the letter, or for that matter anything else. Simply be aware, first of your body and its tensions, then of your breathing and the imagined movement of the color into you and back out of you, and allow your mind to become clear.

After five minutes, change from the fourfold breath to ordinary, slow breathing. Picture in your mind's eye the Coelbren letter you've chosen as a theme, as though it stood hovering in the air in front of you, and begin thinking about what it means. Recall as much of its meaning as you can, and try to see how that unfolds from the sound and the shape of the mouth as the sound is spoken. Add in the color and gematria value of the letter if that seems useful to you. As ideas gather around the letter, consider them in a general way. Then, out of the various insights that come to mind as you think about the letter, choose one and follow it out step by step, thinking about its meaning and implications, taking it as far as you can.

If you're meditating on the Coelbren letter A, for example, the meanings given as starting points include "proceeding forward; continuation in the same state or condition, whether of motion, action, or rest." You might start by considering each of these meanings, one at a time, and see what memories, ideas, or fancies they stir up. Is there something in your present life that seems to be flowing ahead smoothly, or is this something lacking in your world just now? What would it be like if some part of your life that isn't currently in that condition were to start flowing smoothly—and what would you have to do to make that happen?

If you're a student or practitioner of a spiritual or religious tradition, you can certainly integrate symbols, ideas, and insights from that source into your Coelbren meditations. If you don't happen to have such a commitment, though, or if it doesn't feel right to you to bring in material from that source to your work with the Coelbren, don't worry about it. One of the most useful things about the Western way of meditation is that it can be applied to anything, including the most ordinary incidents of your daily life.

Unless you have quite a bit of experience in meditation, your thoughts will likely wander away from the theme again and again. Instead of simply bringing them back in a jump, follow them back through the chain of wandering thoughts until you reach the point where they left the theme. If you're meditating on the Coelbren letter A, for example, and suddenly notice that you're thinking about your grandmother instead, don't simply go back to A and start again. Work your way back. What got you thinking about your grandmother? Memories of a Thanksgiving dinner when you were a child. What called up that memory? Recalling the taste of the roasted mixed nuts she used to put out for the guests. Where did that come from? Thinking about squirrels. Why squirrels? Because you heard the scuttling noise of a squirrel running across the roof above you, and it distracted you from thinking about A.

Whenever your mind strays from the theme, bring it back up the track of wandering thoughts in this same way. This approach has two advantages. First of all, it has much to teach about the way your mind works, the flow of its thoughts, and the sort of associative leaps it habitually makes. Second, it develops the habit of returning to the theme, and with practice you'll find that your thoughts run back to the theme of your meditations just as enthusiastically as they run away from it. Time and regular practice will shorten the distance they run, until eventually your mind learns to run straight ahead along the meanings and implications of a theme without veering from it at all.

To start with, spend ten minutes meditating in this way; when this is easy, go up to fifteen minutes, and if you can spare the time, add five more minutes whenever the period you've set yourself seems too easy. When you're done, repeat the cleansing breath once to close the meditation. Write up the experience in your journal as soon as possible afterwards. Be sure to note down the images and ideas that came up in the meditation since these are likely to prove useful later, in further meditations or in casting and interpreting Coelbren readings.

When meditating with the Coelbren, it's often best to choose a different letter for each day's practice. Start with the letter A, and take a moment to review the discussion of that letter in Chapter Three before starting the meditation. After you finish the fourfold breath and start the meditation itself, imagine the letter in front of you and silently repeat its sound, letting your mouth go into the position you would need to say it aloud. Try to relate the sound and the mouth position to the basic meaning of the letter. Be willing to let your mind rest on the letter, so to speak, as you wait for insights to surface. Meditation can be a lot like fishing—there's sometimes a long wait before something nibbles at the bait.

In your next meditation session, meditate on E in the same way, and so on through the Coelbren. When you've worked your way through the Coelbren alphabet, go back to A again, and review your notes before you start your meditation session. Go on to do the same thing with each letter. Over time, as you meditate your way through the twenty-four letters of the Coelbren and each session adds to those before it, you'll develop a clear personal sense of what each letter means. This will greatly improve your ability to draw meaning from the letters when you're casting and interpreting readings.

Once you have meditated on each of the twenty-four Coelbren letters, consider using the same methods to explore other aspects of Welsh bardic tradition. It can be a fascinating process to go through some of the stories and symbols in *Barddas*, using them as raw material for meditation and seeing if you can find and interpret the many hidden meanings Iolo wove into his work. It can be even more fascinating to work through the Four Branches of the *Mabinogion* in the same way, treating each of these classic Welsh legends as a narrative of the unfolding of the individual soul.

In either of these cases, consider using the tools discussed in Chapter Four to unpack the meanings of the names of people and places included in the narratives. Put the names into Coelbren, interpret them as sequences of letters that each has its own meaning to offer, and check to see what meaning you can extract from the gematria of the word, and you can learn much more than the obvious meaning of the text.

Scrying the Coelbren

Another traditional Western method of meditation uses the imagination, rather than the thinking mind, to unfold the inner meanings of a set of symbols. Carl Jung, the psychologist mentioned in Chapter Four, called this method "active imagination," but it dates from long before Jung's time and has an older name: scrying.

The word "scrying" originally meant seeing in the ordinary sense—the related word "descry," meaning "to sight at a distance", still gets a little use in modern literary English—but "scrying" was adopted many years ago as a term for a very special kind of "seeing" that doesn't rely on the physical eyes. If you've ever daydreamed—and who hasn't?—you've come into contact with the very simplest form of scrying.

The main reason most people don't get beyond that simplest form is the way that modern cultures dismiss the power of the imagination. To call something "imaginary" nowadays is to label it as unreal and unimportant—but there's nothing more real or important than the power of the imagination. Look around you at everything that was made by human beings; every one of those things had to be imagined before it could be made. Someone, or more than likely several someones, saw a need or sensed a desire and imagined something to fill it, and the mental images that resulted from that act of imagination became more and more exact until they could guide the tools of a craftsperson or the machinery of a factory to turn the image into a material reality.

Philosophers and psychologists have shown, though, that the power of the imagination goes even further than this. Though most of us don't notice this most of the time, our five senses don't actually show us a complete picture of the world around us. Instead, they give us a stream of fragmentary sensations: brown, green, rough, smooth, straight, bent, and so on. Only when these glimpses reach our minds are they assembled into a picture, and the activity of the mind that does this is the same one we use when we build up an imagined picture. (The only difference is that when you imagine something, you're getting the fragmentary sensations from your memory rather than directly from your sense organs.) We literally imagine the world into being, building it moment by moment out of the raw material provided by the senses.[55]

When the imagination draws on imagery from memory instead of the senses, the result can be a simple daydream. If this process is approached in certain ways, though, the images can weave themselves into patterns and insights like the ones that can be accessed by divination. This is the secret of scrying: the free play of imagination, pursued in a state of relaxed concentration and gently guided by the will, can open up unexpected realms of inspiration and understanding.

---

[55] See the discussion of this process in Barfield 1965, pp. 19–27.

The practicalities of scrying are much the same as those of meditation: the same posture and the same preliminary practices are used for both. When you scry, you'll take the meditation posture described above, move your awareness through your physical body from the soles of your feet to the top of your head, and then clear your mind with five minutes or so of the fourfold breath, just as though you were about to meditate.

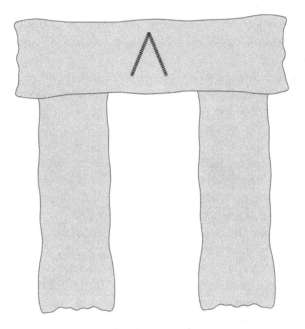

Scrying portal

Next, imagine that you are facing a dolmen arch—the kind of ancient stone arch, made of two standing stones topped by a lintel stone, that was used by the ancients at Stonehenge and elsewhere. The arch stands in front of you, a short distance away. It is large enough for you to step through; for the time being, though, don't look through it. At the center of the lintel stone, above the opening, is carved the Coelbren letter you are going to explore through scrying. Make this image as clear as you can, but don't worry if it's only an image in your mind's eye—that's all it has to be. Some people can make an image like this seem to hover in front of their physical eyes, but if you're not one of those people, that shouldn't stop you from scrying.

Once the dolmen arch is clear in your mind's eye, imagine yourself looking through it. On the other side is a landscape of some sort. Let it take whatever form it wishes, and spend a minute or two letting it take shape in your imagination before going on. Then, slowly and clearly, imagine yourself rising from your chair, walking to the dolmen arch, and passing through it. The portal remains open behind you, and if you look back you can see your physical body sitting in the chair. Look around at the realm beyond the door, and allow yourself to notice as many details as you can.

It's traditional at this stage of scrying to call for an imaginary guide, and then to wait for the guide to appear. Let it appear in whatever form happens to occur to your imagination, whether this is human, animal, or something else. Talk to it and see how it responds. If you're comfortable accepting guidance from it, ask it to show you some of the secrets of the Coelbren letter you're scrying. It will take you on a journey and show you things, and it may also instruct you directly. Ask it any questions you wish, and pay close attention to its answers. Every detail of the landscape around you and every word spoken to you havesomething to teach.

It's important to treat the things you encounter as though they were real, for the duration of the scrying. Some people have trouble doing this—again, our culture's disdain for the human imagination is involved here—but it's important if you want to get the most out of the experience. Like the people and things you encounter in your dreams, the people and things you will meet when scrying seem to have a life of their own, and can say and do things that you may not expect. Behave toward them with this in mind, and they can show you and teach you any number of surprising things.

When the journey or the instruction comes to an end, ask your guide to bring you back to your starting point, and thank it for its guidance. Then return through the dolmen arch, imagine yourself sitting back in the chair where your physical body has been all the while, and then slowly and carefully dissolve the image of the dolmen arch. As it disappears, concentrate on the thought that no unwanted energies or beings can come into your daily life from the realm of the figure you've been scrying. Use a few cycles of fourfold breath to clear your mind, then use the clearing breath to close the scrying. Write up the experience in your Coelbren journal as soon as possible, while the details are still fresh in your mind.

You may find yourself a little disoriented at first after scrying, especially the first few times you do it. If so, eating some food will settle you back down in short order. Routine activities such as washing the dishes can also help reorient your awareness back to the realm of ordinary experience.

Working with scrying

Scrying and meditation can be done independently of each other with good results, but combining the two is far more effective for most people. The key concept here is that each of the things you experience while scrying becomes a theme for a meditation.

After a successful scrying, you may find yourself wanting to do another scrying the next day, but you'll gain more from the experience if you take your time and use meditation to make sense of everything you got from one scrying before going on to the next. For every practice session you spend scrying, plan on spending at least three practice sessions in meditation, exploring the meaning of the things you saw and heard during the scrying.

It's often best to start by drawing up a list of the symbols you encountered in your scrying, so you can then go down the list one meditation session at a time. Let's say, for example, that you scryed the Coelbren letter Li; your guide was a young woman in a brown dress of old-fashioned cut, who led you to a spring below the top of a mountain, and then along the course of the stream that flowed from the spring all the way along its course to the sea. Along the way you saw a salmon in the water, a willow tree with its leaves trailing in the current, seagulls circling in the wind above the seashore, and a coracle—the traditional Welsh boat, made of leather over a wooden frame—pulled up on the sand, with a single oar and a simple plow in it. Your list might run something like this:

Mountain
Spring below the peak
Stream flowing toward the sea
Salmon
Willow with leaves dipping into water
Seagulls
Coracle
Oar
Plow

Each of these can then become a theme for a meditation session. In doing these meditations, call up the imagery from the scrying into your mind's eye, attend to the image for a while, and then ask yourself: what does this have in common with the letter Li? You may not want to let yourself be satisfied with the first answer that comes to mind, either. How far you pursue each symbol is up to you, but most novice scryers run out of patience long before the symbols in their scryings run out of wisdom to offer.

This is not to say that everything in a scrying is necessarily a fount of wisdom. One problem faced by beginners in scrying, especially those who don't have a lot of prior experience with meditation, is that stray thoughts and irrelevancies end up being woven into the scrying by the untrained mind. Like a radio symbol in which the message is mixed with static, scryings by novice scryers often contain a mix of useful material and random imagery. As you meditate on each scrying, keep an eye out for things that seem clearly out of place. Meditate on them anyway, to be sure that you're not missing some unexpected meaning, but be ready to say to yourself, "Okay, that was just noise."

The most important rule for all these practices is simply to take the time you need. If you ever feel that you need another session or two to be sure you understand something, don't ignore that perception. One symbol that's fully opened up through meditation or one scrying that's thoroughly understood will take you further than dozens of each that you've skimmed over lightly and then forgotten.

A final word of caution may be in order here. Scrying can be a powerful tool for deepening your understanding of the Coelbren and opening up the hidden potentials of human awareness, but it can also be an opportunity for many different kinds of foolishness, some of them relatively amusing, some a good deal less so. People have made spectacular blunders by blindly trusting information received from scrying and similar practices in a simplemindedly literal way. The 2012 fiasco, in which tens of thousands of people convinced themselves that the world was going to end on December 21 of that year, was partly driven by this habit. Many of those people either used exercises like scrying themselves, or listened eagerly to the stories of others who did so, and all of them seem to have taken the symbolic images they got in far too literal a sense.

The best way to avoid these pitfalls is to remember that scryings take place in a world of their own, the world of the imagination, and what you experience there may have no more to do with the world where most of us spend our waking hours than, say, the events in a dream. The things you encounter in scrying always need to be assessed according to what contemporary Druid teacher Philip Carr-Gomm calls the three special senses of the Druid: common sense, a sense of proportion, and a sense of humor. If you keep these guides firmly in mind, you're unlikely to go astray.

CHAPTER SEVEN

Coelbren magic

ᚪᚢᚳᚾᛞᛁᚳᚱᚩᚱ

> With the voice was light, and in the light, form; and the voice was in three tones, three vocalizations, pronounced together at the same moment. And in the vision were three forms and colors, which were the form of light; and one with the voice, and the color and form of that voice, were the three first letters.[56]

There seems to be no evidence that Iolo Morganwg practiced magic. Nor, as far as anyone knows, did any of the bards who studied with him take up that strange and little-understood art. Partly this was simply a matter of chronology, since Iolo lived and died before Eliphas Lévi launched the modern magical revival with his famous 1855 volume *Dogme et Rituel de la Haute Magie* (*Doctrine and Ritual of High Magic*). Partly, too, Iolo's improbable success as the restorer of bardic institutions and champion of a Welsh past that never happened depended in large part on the support of Christian clergy in the Anglican and Unitarian traditions, and none of those clergymen would have tolerated Iolo's teachings for a moment if those had included the practice of magic.

---

[56] Williams ab Ithel 2004, p. 47.

Yet human beings have practiced magic since long before the beginning of recorded history, and most of them have had no trouble reconciling their magical practice with their religious faith. This was as true in Iolo's lifetime as it was centuries before then, and it is still true today. Nor is magic purely a habit of people in Pagan faiths: there are rich and thoroughly developed traditions of Christian magic, for example. The ancient Druids from whom Iolo claimed to inherit some aspects of his bardic lore were famous in classical times for their mastery of magic, and many modern students of Druidry and Celtic spirituality practice magic today.

What is magic? Dion Fortune, one of the great twentieth-century authors of books on magic, defined it as "the art and science of causing change in consciousness in accordance with will." That definition is more subtle than it looks, because it doesn't specify whose consciousness is being changed, or for that matter whose will it is in accordance with! A religious mystic who seeks to bring her consciousness into perfect harmony with the Divine will fits this definition just as precisely as an ordinary practitioner of folk magic who wants to make some part of his life go a little more smoothly. The flexibility of the definition isn't accidental, partly because Dion Fortune was herself a Christian mystic as well as a very capable practitioner of magic, and partly because Fortune had encountered many forms and methods of magic and had a good grasp of the raw diversity of magical practice.

To make sense of the definition, it's important to realize that mages—practitioners of magic—don't see the universe as a collection of dead matter floating meaninglessly in empty space, the way that believers in modern materialist philosophies so often do. To mages, the universe is alive and conscious, and so is everything in it. Some things are more obviously full of life and consciousness than others, of course. It requires a keenly developed awareness to sense the hidden life and consciousness sleeping in a stone, for example. Yet mages sense that presence in stones and everything else.

The practice of magic is thus among other things a way to become aware of the life and consciousness within all things. It is also a way of working with life and consciousness, however. Just as divination enables you to listen to the messages the world is sending you, magic enables you to send messages of your own, and in that way, influence the course of events in yourself and in the world. Magic is the process of entering into a conversation with the world and asking it for a favor from time to time. The most important tools for doing this are symbols.

Symbols in magic

Ask someone who doesn't practice magic what tools mages use, and you'll probably hear a lot about wands, pentacles, and similar pieces of hardware. Ask an experienced mage what tools mages use, by contrast, and symbols are likely to come up first.

The wands that some mages use make good examples of a symbol. The wand is a symbol of the element of fire. It represents all the meanings that the idea of "fire" brings to mind, and in particular, the active will and energy of the mage. Part of its symbolism is geometrical—a wand is a straight line, after all, and like any other straight line it symbolizes the unity and directed nature of the will. To point a wand at something is symbolically to direct your will and energy at that thing. To draw a symbol in the air with a wand is to let your will and energy flow into that symbol. To pick up the wand is to focus your will and energy, and to put the wand back down is to relax that focus.

You can do quite a bit with a single symbol, and a little later in this chapter, we'll discuss one of the simpler ways in which this is done. In the more advanced forms of magical practice, however, mages use whole constellations of symbols, all of them focusing on the same set of meanings. Colors, numbers, shapes, sounds, scents—the range of possible symbols is as wide as the reach of the human senses. Among the most common symbols used in magical practice, however, are the letters or characters used in ordinary writing.

That practice goes back at least as far as ancient Egypt, where priests and priestesses used hieroglyphics as symbols in their magical workings. Taoist mages use Chinese characters as magical symbols, Hindu mages use the letters of the Sanskrit syllabary,[57] and in Japan the *hiragana* syllabary and several other writing systems are put to work in the rich tradition of *kotodama* word-magic. In Western magical traditions, the letters of the Hebrew alphabet have seen a great deal of use as magical symbols, and so have less familiar alphabets such as Enochian and Theban. The runes, the sacred script of the old Norse and Germanic cultures, were magical symbols before they were used for ordinary writing.

The letters of the Coelbren are well suited for the same purpose. Each one, as we have already seen, represents a particular energy or quality,

---

[57] A syllabary is a set of letters which each represents a syllable, the way the letters in an alphabet represent sounds.

expressed in its sound. Divination reads each Coelbren as an indication of the energy or quality of some part of a present or future situation. Meditation provides a deeper understanding of each energy or quality. Magic takes the energy or quality of a letter or a sequence of letters, and projects it into a situation where it would be helpful but is not yet present.

Thus it's important to practice divination and meditation with the Coelbren letters before trying to use them in magic. You need to have a clear understanding of what the letters mean and how they relate to the world around you before you use them in magic. Once you have a well-developed sense of what each letter means and what kind of events in your life it represents, you can begin to put the letters to magical use to improve your own life and those of the people around you.

Divination and meditation are important in another sense, however. Ethics are important in magic—even more important, in fact, than they are in the rest of life. That importance unfolds from one of the simple facts of magic: any energy or quality you try to project into anything else passes through your own consciousness, and leaves some of itself behind. One of my teachers used to call this the Raspberry Jam Principle: in using magic, just as in handling raspberry jam, you can't spread it on anything else without getting some on yourself.

Thus it's vital to be sure that you're prepared to cope with the energies you invoke when they show up in your own life, as they certainly will. The best ways to take care of this essential first step, in turn, are divination and meditation. Before you decide to do any magical working, always cast and interpret a Coelbren reading to find out if the working is a good idea. (The three rays of light spread or the Gwydion and the pigs spread are both good choices for this.) Then meditate on the answer you get, and be very sure you understand the answer and will accept the consequences it predicts for you.

One rule is worth following strictly: don't use magic on another person unless you have their permission to do so. Consent is just as important in magic as it is in sex, and for similar reasons. Trying to force your influence on someone against their will is a bad idea no matter how it's done, and if you do this with magic, the blowback is not something you want to deal with.

In general, you will find that the most effective way to work with magic is to use it to change yourself, rather than trying to change other people. If you're lonely and want a loving relationship, for example, don't try to use magic to get someone to love you—this reliably blows up in messy ways. Instead, use magic to make yourself more lovable. (The letter Hi is very useful for this, and so is Gi, which will bring you into contact and interaction with people who may be interested in you.) If you don't have as much money as you want, similarly, don't use magic to try to get the world to give it to you for free—use magic to make yourself aware of opportunities you can use to earn more. (The letter Ci is an excellent choice here, and so is Pi, which will help you transform vague desires into focused ambition and get you moving toward your goal.)

Any time you can frame the goal of your magical workings in terms of making changes in yourself, do it. You'll find that the results of this kind of magical work are better and more lasting than you can expect if you do things the clumsy way, and try to force other people or circumstances to do what you want.

Simple Coelbren magic

Magical workings range from the very simple to the very complex, and the Coelbren can be used at any point along that spectrum. To get you started in your explorations, here is a simple method of using the letters to work magic.

To use this method, you'll need to learn and practice a special method of breathing called "pore breathing." Sit in your meditation position and go through the preliminary relaxation, letting go of all unnecessary tension. Then breathe in slowly and deeply. As you do this, imagine that instead of breathing in through your nostrils, you are drawing in air through the pores of your skin all over your body. Feel the air flowing into you and filling your whole body. Pause for a little while, and then breathe out and imagine the air flowing out through your pores in exactly the same way that it flowed in. Repeat the process, and keep doing it for five minutes or so. Practice this daily until you get a good clear sense of air flowing in and out through the pores in your skin when you choose to feel this.

What is flowing in and out through your pores is not actually air, of course. It is the life force, the secret power behind magic. If you've read about martial arts, yoga, or many forms of spirituality, you already know about the life force. It's not something materialists in the modern world like to talk about, but it has names in languages around the world—*qi* in Chinese, *prana* in Sanskrit, *ruach* in Hebrew, and so on.[58] The old Welsh word *nwyfre*, pronounced "noo-IV-ruh," is one of its many names, and this name is commonly used in many of today's Druid traditions, including those that trace their lineage back to Iolo Morganwg.

By breathing nwyfre into your body through your pores, you charge yourself with the life force. By breathing it out again, you expel aspects of the life force that no longer benefit you. You can use pore breathing for this purpose, drawing in clean nwyfre to fill your body with life and vitality, and breathing out imbalances and impurities. Try it! Seven pore breaths each day, breathing in life and breathing out waste products, can improve your physical and mental health, and this practice is also good basic training for Coelbren magic.

To take the next step, you'll need to learn and practice another skill. This is the art of charging the space around you with the energies of a Coelbren letter. Let's take the letter A for example. Imagine it as clearly as possible in the air in front of you, and think about what it means: steady, relaxed onward movement, like a great river flowing through its valley toward the sea. Now imagine that meaning as a quality in the air around you. Feel it as strongly as you can: strong, patient, unhurried, irresistible, moving toward its goal without meeting any obstacle. While you're doing this, imagine that the air around you is the color associated with A—sky blue. All your previous practice with color breathing will come in handy here!

Now begin a variation on the pore breathing you've practiced. As you breathe in, imagine the feeling of the letter A, and the sky blue light surrounding you, as it flows into your body. As you breathe out, the nwyfre flows out through your pores but the feeling remains. Breathe in again, and more of the feeling of A flows into you; breathe out again, leaving the feeling in you. Repeat this a total of seven times, until all the feeling of the letter A is concentrated in your body and none of it remains around you. Then reverse the process; breathe in, bringing in plain nwyfre through your pores, and breathe out, letting some of the feeling of the letter flow out of you. Repeat until you have done seven pore breaths and all the feeling of the letter is outside you again. Practice this every day until you can do it easily.

---

[58] Yes, it's also "the Force" in those famous science fiction movies. George Lucas borrowed the concept from the Japanese martial arts, where it's called *ki*.

This exercise is also the simplest form of Coelbren magic. If you need the quality or energy of one of the Coelbren letters in some situation in your life, breathe in one of the letters seven times as just described and leave the energy of the letter inside you while you deal with the situation. Later—if necessary, hours or days later—breathe it out again. For example, if you need calm and confidence in dealing with a difficult task, breathe in the energy of the letter A and let its steady unruffled flow carry you smoothly to your goal.

If you have to deal with a person who tries to get emotional reactions out of you, breathe in the energy of the letter Y to keep yourself impartial and uninvolved. If you need to focus all your attention on something and set aside all distractions, breathe in the energy of Ni, and so on. (As an exercise, meditate on each of the letters and see how many situations you can think of where that letter's energy would be helpful to you.)

What if you need to influence someone or something else? That's more complex, but you can learn how to do it once you've practiced the basic method just given, to the point that you can get good results with it. The method for influencing other people and things begins in the same way as the basic method, by breathing energy into yourself. Once you have done this, the next phase of the work begins.

Let's imagine that someone has asked you to help them be calm and confident during some situation they're facing. You breathe in the energy of the letter A as described above. Once you have done this, begin breathing the energy out of you, but this time don't do it through the pores all over your body. Raise your hands and turn them to face each other as though you were holding a ball in front of your chest. Breathe the energy of the letter out through the palms of your hands, and not through any other part of your body. As it flows out through your palms it forms a ball of A-energy. Feel the ball between your hands, and picture it as a glowing ball of sky-blue light. The more clearly you can imagine it, the more effective the working will be.

Once you have breathed all the energy of the letter into the ball of light between your hands, and none of it remains in your body, send it to the person you want to help. At first, it's easiest to do this if the other person is physically present. Have them sit facing you, and when the ball of energy is charged, push it toward them and imagine it flowing into their body and filling them. If possible, the other person should imagine the same thing. Later on, when you've practiced this kind of magic often enough that it's easy for you, you can do it for someone who isn't present. In this case you'll need to imagine the ball of letter energy flying across the distance to wherever the other person is, reaching them, and flowing into their body.

Coelbren talismans

The method just described can also be used as a simple but effective way to make and charge Coelbren talismans. A talisman is an object that has been charged with the life force so that it radiates a magical influence. Once charged, it keeps on working until it runs out of the life force. Talismans are thus very well suited to any situation where you need some specific energy to keep acting in your life for a long time.

Every talisman needs four things. The first is a *material basis*—that is, some kind of physical substance that will hold a charge of nwyfre the way a battery holds electricity. The second is an *appropriate symbol*—that is, something that represents the intention, and can be drawn, carved, painted, or otherwise placed in or on the material basis. The third is a *conscious intention*—that is, something specific that you want the talisman to do. The fourth is a *magical consecration*—that is, a way of putting the life force into the material basis so that the talisman has energy to work with.

For the material basis of a Coelbren talisman, you can use many substances. The best in most situations is wood, which holds charges of nwyfre very well. An ebill made according to the instructions in Chapter Three would be the best possible material basis for a Coelbren talisman, but not everyone has the time or the woodworking skills to make ebillion! Any small piece of wood into which you can carve, cut, paint, or draw a Coelbren letter will make a suitable material basis for a talisman. A short twig, or a piece of wood an inch long and a fraction of an inch wide and deep, is quite adequate.

If you have access to different kinds of wood, you can certainly choose the type to fit the purpose of the talisman—for example, oak is a traditional symbol of strength and thus would be well suited for a talisman of Ri or Fi, while willow represents flexibility and gentleness and so would be better suited for talismans of Hi or Li. If you live in a city and your only access to wood is through a local craft store, however, or from fallen twigs from a tree in the street outside your home, use what you can find.

Just as the Coelbren letters were sometimes written on stone (and then called Coelfaen), you can use a small stone for a talisman, since stone is extremely good at holding charges of nwyfre. (That's why ancient peoples raised standing stones and later peoples built stone temples: in both cases, the stone absorbed the energies of religious rituals and radiated blessings in the area for months and years thereafter.) Engraving stones takes a certain amount of specialized equipment, and if you want to use this method to carve your Coelfaen letters, you should probably find someone to teach you how to do it, or look up the process in books. If you want to use a simpler process, on the other hand, paint or permanent markers can be used equally well. Other materials are also an option, though you may need to experiment—or read up on the subject in other books on magic—to see which of them will hold a charge of nwyfre well.

The material basis, then, can be provided in any of these ways. The appropriate symbol is provided by the Coelbren letter you have chosen. The next step is the conscious intention.

Supposing that you wanted to make a talisman of the letter A, for example, you would start by deciding exactly what you want it to accomplish. Your intention needs to be put in a single phrase or sentence. It should be simple and straightforward, and it should avoid using negatives—words like "no," "not," and "without." Your intention should always state what you want, not what you don't want. It can be very simple: "Calm and confidence," for example, would be a good intention for a talisman of the letter A. It can be wise to choose the intention before you settle on the appropriate letter to use for symbolism—it sometimes happens that once you choose your intention, it becomes clear that you need to use a different letter from the one you originally selected.

The final step, the magical consecration, can be handled in many ways, but the simplest of them uses a variation on the method of pore breathing and charging you have already learned. This is done in much the same way as the second method given above, for charging other people, except you charge your talisman instead. Start by speaking your intention aloud seven times. Next, charge the air with the energy and color of A, and then breathe it into yourself through your pores seven times, gathering the energy in yourself. If this is convenient, do this sitting at a desk or table with the talisman in front of you.

Then breathe the energy out seven times through the palms of your hands. Instead of forming a ball in the air, project it from your palms into your talisman. Imagine it flowing into the talisman and being completely absorbed by the wood or stone. Once you have breathed all of the energy out of yourself and into the talisman, the talisman is charged, and will radiate your intention for months to come. If your intention is something that will take a long time to accomplish, you can charge the talisman again at intervals; the sixth day of the moon—that is, seven days after the day of the new moon, since the day of the new moon itself doesn't count in the traditional reckoning—is a good day to do this.

Coelbren sigil magic

The methods of Coelbren magic discussed above are very basic, though they can be quite effective in ordinary use. If you want to go on to more advanced magical methods using the Coelbren, you will need to learn much more about magic than this book can teach you. Just like playing a musical instrument or using a martial art in combat, effective magic takes quite a bit of study and practice. It's not something you can just pick up and do with no prior experience!

Magic can, however, be learned from books, provided that you are willing to put in the time and effort needed to follow the course of study in a good magical textbook. My books *The Celtic Golden Dawn* and *The Druid Magic Handbook* cover two different systems of magic that are entirely compatible with the Coelbren, for example, and there are many books by other authors that can also provide you with detailed instruction. Most of the practical applications of Coelbren magic can be worked out easily enough once you see how other sets of symbols are used in whatever system of magic you decide to study.

One magical technique that may not be obvious to those without substantial background in occult studies, but can be learned quickly and added to other systems, is the use of sigils drawn on a matrix of letters to represent names and words of power. If you know your way around Renaissance magic you may be familiar with the way that names and words are turned into sigils using the magic squares of the planets, and students of Golden Dawn magic will be familiar with sigils drawn on the rose from the Rose Cross lamen. The same thing can be done with the Coelbren once they are placed in a matrix of 5 × 5 spaces, as shown below. (Since there are twenty-four letters, the central space is filled with the emblem of the three rays of light.)

Coelbren sigils 1

There are many possible matrices for the Coelbren, of course. This one is based on the traditional order in which the Coelbren alphabet was created, and you will find it especially useful for any magical work that involves creating things, conditions, or patterns in your life. Other matrices can be devised and used for other purposes. You may find it useful, as you proceed with your own Coelbren meditations, to devise your own matrices and use them to create sigils that are unique to your own work.

To trace a sigil from this or any other matrix, take any name or word of power you intend to use in a magical working. Imagine the matrix in the air before you, and with your finger or a symbolic working tool such as a wand or staff, trace out a zigzag line on the matrix that starts at the first letter of the name and goes to each of the other letters in turn.

For example, if you intend to invoke the ancient Celtic god Mabon, a Coelbren sigil can be part of the ritual of invocation. When you reach the point in the invocation where tracing the sigil is appropriate, imagine the matrix before you and point with your finger or working tool at the letter Mi. Go from there to A, to Bi, to O, and to Ni, as shown below.

Coelbren sigils 2

Simple as it seems, this technique is highly effective in practice, and may be combined with any of the other technical methods of ceremonial magic. Students of my books *The Celtic Golden Dawn* and *The Mysteries of Merlin* will find it particularly well suited to use in the rituals given in those volumes, where the names of Celtic gods are invoked.

Further possibilities

The handful of magical techniques given in this chapter are only a very small subset of the possible range of uses for the Coelbren in magic. Now that the key to the meanings of the Coelbren letters has been recovered and the letters can be used again for divination, meditation, and magic, any number of other possibilities are open to the student. Consider taking up this challenge, and breaking new ground with the Coelbren.

Summary of the divinatory Coelbren

ᛠᚢᚲᛄᛞᛁᚴᚱᚩᚱ

Letter	Welsh word	Meaning
ᛠ	a, and	Proceeding forward, continuation in the same state or condition, whether of motion, action, or rest.
ᚢ	–	Motion checked, interrupted, or broken, an indirect, negative, or distorted condition.
ᛁ	i, into	The movement of a thing to its proper place, being or becoming a part of a whole, approach, subordination.
ᚢ	o, from	Movement outward or away from, departure, rejection or projection, casting or putting forth.
ᚢ	–	Sorting or distributing things into different classes or categories, discrimination, divergence, choosing.
ᛉ	y, the	A state or condition of balance or suspension, neutrality, pause, impartiality or uninvolvement.

Y	–	Wholeness, completeness, unity, the background or context in which other things or actions have their place.
 �	bi, will be	The being of any thing in a quiescent state, a condition or state of being, mere existence, perception.
<	ci, dog	Holding, containing, comprehending, reaching or extension toward a thing, catching, attaining and apprehending.
>	di, without	Expanding, unfolding, laying open, distribution and division, the opposite of Ci.
 ᚠ	–	Causation, impulsion, setting a thing or action in motion, the source or initial impetus of change or activity.
 ᚲ	gi, tendon	Attachment, cohesion, appetite, desire, and also compensation and mutual reaction of things on each other.
ᚻ	hi, she	Generation, abundance, fertility, nurturance and support, response favorable to an external cause or stimulus.
 ᚼ	–	Flow, softness, smoothness, lightness, open space, solution or evanescence, movement without effort, as gliding.
 ᚹ	mi, I	Comprehending, embracing, or surrounding; enclosure or capacity, inclusion within something; large or complex.
 ᚾ	ni, not	Distinguishing or identifying something; an individual object or subject; something new, simple, or small.
 ᚱ	pi, magpie	Pushing, penetrating, springing or putting forth; a protrusion or prominence, sharpness, convexity.
 ᚱ	rhi, king	Force, prevalence, or superiority; an action performed by main strength; excess, tearing or breaking, causing damage.

ᚱ   si, murmur   Inferiority, secrecy, privacy; a secret or private knowledge or indication; insinuation, indirect action.

↑   –   Tension, drawing, or straining; stretching or drawing out; bringing to an end; confinement or termination.

ᚦ   –   Realm, extent, or field of action; territory; boundary, or surface, marking the limit of a given force or influence.

ᚾ   lli, flood   Turbulence, confusion, and disruption; difficulty in proceeding; obstacles, solidity, movement requires effort.

ᚤ   fe, he   Protection, limitation, discipline, establishment of order; response unfavorable to an external cause or stimulus.

ᚲ   –   Conflict, difficulty, opposition, obstacle; interference between two or more contending forces or things.

The Coelbren
and *The Celtic Golden Dawn*

ΛɅ<↓>ΙΛΓΟΓ

Ironically, the discovery of the meanings of the Coelbren came just too late for me to include Iolo's alphabet in a project that would have benefited immensely from it. As mentioned in the introduction to this book, my studies of the Coelbren go back many years, but I began the researches that resulted in this book shortly after completing work on *The Celtic Golden Dawn*. That book, which was published in 2013, was my attempt to reverse engineer an intriguing but vanished system of alternative spirituality—a fusion of the teachings of the nineteenth-century Hermetic Order of the Golden Dawn and the traditions of the eighteeenth- and nineteenth-century Druid Revival to which Iolo Morganwg contributed so much. Orders that accomplished this unlikely but effective fusion flourished in Britain during the first half of the twentieth century, but they disappeared during and after the Second World War.

I had not yet discovered the *Dosparth Ederyn Dafod Aur* when I wrote *The Celtic Golden Dawn*, and so didn't have the opportunity to incorporate the Coelbren into the symbolism and lore of the system I created for that book. I was startled to discover, though, that the Coelbren fit perfectly into the system I had assembled, and adds substantially to the possibilities of the system. While the Coelbren can certainly be used in the ways outlined in this book without reference to that broader symbolism, those readers who are interested in the system of *The Celtic Golden Dawn*, or are familiar with esotericism generally, may find the following correspondences of interest. The names of the spheres and the geomantic figures are Welsh rather than Hebrew in the one case and Latin in the other, for reasons explained in *The Celtic Golden Dawn*.

Letter	Tarot card	Geomantic figure	Cabalistic sphere or path
∧	XIX, The Sun	Bendith Fawr	Muner, the Sixth Sphere
⅃	XV, The Devil	Carchar	Naf, the Tenth Sphere
I	XVII, The Star	Elw	Byth, the Eighth Sphere
◇	XVIII, The Moon	Colled	Byw, the Seventh Sphere
V	XVI, The Tower	Cyswllt	Ner, the Ninth Sphere
Y	XX, Judgment	–	Modur, the Fifth Sphere
 Y	XXI, The World	–	Ener, the Fourth Sphere
 L	0, The Fool	Pen y Ddraig	First Path, Naf to Ner
<	I, The Magician	Ffordd	Second Path, Naf to Byth
>	II, The High Priestess	Pobl	Fourth Path, Naf to Byw
 �	III, The Empress	Merch	Third Path, Ner to Byth
 ⟨	IV, The Emperor	Mab	Fifth Path, Ner to Byw

Letter	Tarot card	Geomantic figure	Cabalistic sphere or path
ᚲ	VI, The Lovers	Bendith Fach	Sixth Path, Byth to Byw
ᚴ	V, The Hierophant	Llosgwrn y Ddraig	Seventh Path, Ner to Muner
ᚹ	VII, The Chariot	Coch	Eighth Path, Byth to Muner
ᚺ	IX, The Hermit	Gwyn	Ninth Path, Byw to Muner
ᚱ	VIII, Strength	Tristwch	Tenth Path, Byth to Modur
ᚱ	XI, Justice	–	Eleventh Path, Muner to Modur
ᚱ	X, Wheel of Fortune	Llawenydd	Twelfth Path, Byw to Ener
↑	XII, Hanged Man	–	Thirteenth Path, Muner to Ener
ᚦ	XIV, Temperance	–	Fourteenth Path, Modur to Ener
ᚾ	–	–	Fifteenth Path, Muner to Dofydd
ᛒ	–	–	Seventeenth Path, Muner to Perydd
ᚴ	XIII, Death	–	Twentieth Path, Muner to Celi

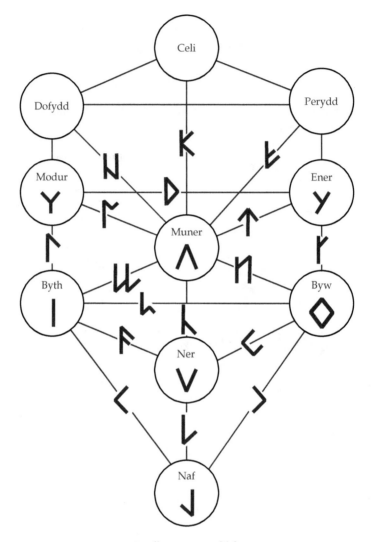

Coelbren tree of life

Selections from *Dosparth Ederyn Dafod Aur*

∧⌵<⌄⌄ᛁ⋀ᚱᛟᚱ

John Williams ab Ithel's discussion of the Coelbren in the commentary on his translation of *Dosparth Ederyn Dafod Aur* is of more than historical value. He devoted many decades of his life to the study of the Coelbren and his comments sum up their history and meaning with a great deal of clarity, illustrated with examples from the Welsh language and bits of tradition from the Christian scriptures he studied as an Anglican minister. I have reprinted his description of the meanings of the sixteen oldest letters here.[59]

Names and natural expressions of the primitive letters

It would appear that the Celtic tongue has retained, in an uncommon degree, traces of that natural mode in which language was first formed—when objects were presented to the eyes of our first parent "to see what he could call them" (Genesis 2:19). This may account for the bardic tradition that the Cymraeg was spoken by Enos, and perpetuated beyond the deluge by Japheth and his posterity, when the other languages were corrupted at Babel.

---

[59] These may be found in Williams ab Ithel 1856, pp. 13–18.

The various sounds of letters appear evidently to have been produced by the natural and spontaneous effort of man in his primitive state to express ideas.

The names of the Welsh vowels fully signify the ideas intended. As the consonants, however, cannot be articulated without a vocalic sound attached to them, they were anciently called by the name which their respective powers, followed by I, uttered, though the sound really emitted in the effort to express any idea seems to have been somewhat like the short obscure *e* before *r* in final syllables of English words.

A

This power is uttered by opening the lips, and the interior part of the mouth, moderately, and evenly, and breathing firmly, freely, and steadily, from the larynx, while the tongue rests in its natural situation, at the bottom of the mouth.

By this oral gesture, and this open, uninterrupted sound, men may be conceived naturally and spontaneously to have expressed the idea of a *tendency forwards—positive continuance*, in a uniform state, whether of motion, of action, or of rest.

Accordingly A, the sound produced, which is also the name of the letter, constitutes, moreover, a complete term, conveying the general idea of *proceeding, going forth, tending forwards—a positive agency*, or *state*; e.g., "Ev a â Edwart, ev â'i adar" (L. Glyn Cothi) Edward will go, or proceed forth, etc.

E

Let this power be uttered immediately after, or alternately with, an open A, and it will be found that all the organs of speech retain the same position, except that your tongue is now bent forcibly toward the roof of the palate, as if it were intended by nature to arrest or check the egress and free passage of breath.

It is, therefore, diametrically opposite to A. Instead of representing uniform and free continuance of motion, or agency, a direct or positive statement or tendency, it seems naturally to express a *sudden check, motion, or act interrupted, or broken*, an *indirect, perverted*, or *negative state* or *tendency*.

Its name is its own sound E, which is also found to express ideas contrary to those conveyed by A, e.g, *Ang*, strait, narrow, confined; *E-ang*, wide, spacious, ample; *Ofn*, fear; *E-ofn*, bold, intrepid.

I

In uttering this tone, or sound, the tongue is thrust forwards, till it rests against the lower teeth, at the same time it closes the whole interior of the mouth, except a confined and a direct passage for breath along the middle of the palate.

By this oral gesture, and the sound it produces, might naturally be described the *application* or *direction* of a thing to its *proper object*, or *place*. A being or becoming *appropriate* or *internal*, what *approaches*, is *applicable, subservient*, or *inherent*.

The Bards named this letter by the mere repetition of its power, which implies *to, into, for, towards, pertaining to*; as i ffordd, into a road, way; i ddyn, to or for a man; i lawr, towards the flat surface downwards. Mai i mi, there is pertaining to me.

When used without an external object or direction, it refers to self, as "Gweleis i," I saw, as to myself.

O

In uttering this power, alternately with the preceding, the organs of speech entirely reverse their position. The tongue which, in pronouncing *i*, advanced to the teeth, almost closed up the mouth, and confined the breath to a direct and narrow passage, is now *retracted*; retires from the palate, and leaves the way open. The lips, at the same time, are forcibly projected outwards, with a large and circular opening. The whole mouth is thus adjusted, as nature itself would dispose it, for the act of vomiting, or casting forth.

By this gesture, and its correspondent sound, an idea diametrically opposed to that of I would be spontaneously expressed—a *casting, yielding*, or *putting forth*—an *emanation*, or *projection*, from a certain thing; instead of application, direction, or relation to a peculiar object.

The power of this letter, which constitutes its Bardic name, has accordingly in the Cymraeg appropriations, exactly contrasted to those of I; as I, *to, for, towards, into, pertaining to*; O, *of, from, out of, resulting from*.

The inflections of vowels do not come under this rule; they are evidently a corruption of the language, such as would have answered the design of confusion at Babel, though they are now recognized as a system.

B

This articulation is formed by an easy and a natural opening of the mouth, without any forcible impulse of breath, or protrusion of the lips, or any other vocal organ.

It may, therefore, be naturally applied to express the idea of simple perception—the being of any thing in a quiescent state or condition, and hence receive the following appropriations—*being, to be, thing,* or *what is, condition* or *state of being.*

Its name, in the Bardic Alphabet, is Bi, a term which signifies *will be.*

C

This letter is pronounced by fixing the root of the tongue firmly against the root of the palate, so as entirely to fill and close up the interior part of the mouth, till breath forces its way with strong impulse.

Such an oral gesture, and its correspondent sound, naturally attend every effort to hold or contain a large mass with both arms, and also to *catch, reach,* or *touch* a distant object.

This term, therefore, is not limited to the expression of one simple idea; but naturally describes a *holding, containing,* or *comprehending*—a *reaching, touching,* or *catching*—*attaining to,* or *apprehending.*

Its Bardic name is Ci, a term by which we distinguish a dog, on account of its aptitude to catch and hold. "Nerth ci yn y ddant."[60]

D

The articulation of this letter is formed and uttered by closing the edges of the tongue to the upper gums, throughout their whole extent, and suddenly laying it open.

We may, therefore, consider this power as descriptive naturally of expanding, spreading, unfolding, laying open, distribution, or division.

---

[60] "A dog's strength is in its teeth."

Its Bardic name is Di, a term used of old for the Deity, also for *day*— *what unfolds, lays open*. It is evidently a modification of *Dy* the augmentative prefix, rather than the privative *di*.

G

In hugging a substance with the arms, and as it were forcibly adhering to it, we acquire additional power by placing the tongue in the same position as that in which the letter C is pronounced, but as this action is of a less protrusive nature than that of catching or holding, breath is not propelled with new force, and the sound of G is produced.

It may then be considered to have a natural aptitude to describe the ideas of *appetite*, a *grasp, adhesion, mutual attachment, compensation*.

Its bardic name is Gi, which implies a sinew or tendon—the cause of connection and cohesion in the joints.

L

This power, whether expressed in English words, or aspirated, as the ll, is formed by fixing the tip of the tongue against the upper gums, while both sides of it hang open, suffering the air to be *poured out*, and equally dispersed, through all the extremities of the mouth. Such an act of the vocal organs naturally accompanies the act of throwing open the hand and the arms, to describe *solution, effusion, evanescence, open space, gliding, softness, smoothness, levity*.

The Bardic name of the letter is Li, which conveys the ideas above specified; as Lli, *flux* or *flood, stream, effusion of that which is fluid, guiding element*. Llif (lli-af), a *flood, deluge*. Llifo, to *flow, overflow*.

M

If it were attempted to describe naturally, by means of the organs of speech, that one substance was entirely shut up, inclosed, and comprehended in another, the lips would close together, the cheeks would swell moderately, into the imitation of *capacity*, and breath would endeavor to attract notice by sounding the power of M through the nostrils.

M is, therefore, a natural expression of *comprehending, embracing*, or *surrounding*.

Its Bardic name is Mi, *that which is in*, or *identical, myself.* This is the root of mid, an *inclosure, a vessel of capacity*; midd, *an inclosed place.*

N

When we put forth the hand, or extend the finger, to discriminate a simple or minute object, the eye is naturally directed the same way; we look steadfastly at that which we wish another to observe. The tongue at the same instant spontaneously mimics the action of the hand and the eye, by thrusting forward its point in the same direction, till it rests against the upper gums. The breath, being denied a passage through the mouth, tends toward the same spot, through the nostrils, with the sound of N.

This sound is, then, a natural interjection for *look! lo there!* and it is naturally answered by M, *I observe*, or *comprehend.*

We may thus regard the power N as a natural expression of an *object, subject, thing produced*, or *new, discriminated* or *simplified*—the *self-same, simple, small.* Hence its prominent position in the article of the Erse dialect.

Its Bardic name is Ni, which primarily means a *particular thing.* Its negative signification, not, occurs by the same kind of figure which produced ελαχιστα from ελαχιστος, and *minime* from *minimus.*[61]

P

A person desirous of communicating the idea of pushing, would place his body in an inclining posture, his hands would be protruded, his lips pressed together, and forced outward, as in the very act of the impulse described, and the puffing sound of P would be uttered.

The most obvious gesture also to convey the idea of *plumpness, protuberance*, or *convexity*, is to swell and puff out the cheeks, till the articulation is produced.

P may, therefore, be regarded as naturally descriptive of *springing, putting forth, pushing, penetrating, prominence, convexity.* Its name in the

---

[61] The first two of these words are Greek, the second two Latin; in both cases an adjective meaning "very little" evolved into an adverb meaning "not at all."

Bardic alphabet is Pi, which signifies the *magpie*, q.d. the *pricker*.[62] It is the root of pic, a *dart*, pig, a *beak*, and pid, a *point*.

PH[63]

In uttering this sound the organs of speech are not put into complete contact, at the point of articulation, as in the case of P. Some portion of breath escapes, and vibrates in the interstice. It accordingly expresses ideas of like nature with, but less powerful than those of the preceding.

Its Bardic name is Phi, which signifies the act of *casting off, putting forth*. Phy, *aptness to move, to impel*; it is used as a prefix in the composition of words denoting *agency or cause*.

R

This sound is produced by fixing the sides of the tongue firmly against those of the palate, and forcing out the breath in front, so as to cause a rough and strong vibration, between the tip of the tongue, and the upper gums. Its mechanical production is a direct contrast to that of L.

By this energetic power the first linguists would naturally describe *force, prevalence*, or *superiority*; a *motion*, or *action performed by main strength—rubbing, tearing, pervading, breaking*.

Its Bardic name is Rhi or Ri, which implies a king, a chief, a ruler. Rhy is *too much, excessive—prevalent, over*. "Nid da rhy o ddim."[64]

S

When a man designs naturally to point out some particular object, so as not to attract general observation, the point of his tongue drops downwards, and rests against the lower teeth. The upper teeth close over it, as it were, to conceal the unavowed design, and the low, insinuating, hissing sound of S is produced.

This power is, therefore, naturally descriptive of *secret discrimination, insinuation*, a *private marking*, and *distinguishing*.

---

[62] Q.d.: *quid denotat*, "which denotes."
[63] Spelled Ff in modern Welsh but Ph in the formal literary Welsh of Williams ab Ithel's time.
[64] "Not too much of anything."

Its Bardic name is Si, which implies a *hissing* expression of contempt. Si-arad, or Si-arawd, *prating, backbiting,* from Si and arawd, *speech, eloquence*—Si-brwd, a *low murmur,* or *whisper,* from Si and brud, an account or chronicle.

T

In tugging or drawing a line forcefully, the tongue is applied firmly and spontaneously to the fore part of the palate, or upper gums, and forces out a vehement articulation of T.

This power, therefore, naturally describes *tension, drawing,* or *straining,* in whatever manner; *extension, stretching,* or *drawing out. Intension,* or *drawing tight* or *close. Drawing* a line or bound round anything— *confining, straitening, limiting, circumscribing.*

Its Bardic name is Ti, the meaning of which can be perceived in Tid (ti-ad) *a chain;* tid-aw *to tether, tie,* or *confine,* with a line, chain, &c.

APPENDIX 4

Coelbren gematria

ᚾᚢᚳᚫᚦᛁᚴᚱᛟᚱ

The following list of names and words with their gematria values includes most of the important terms from *Barddas*, a selection of important personal and place names from the Four Branches of the *Mabinogion*, and certain other terms from Welsh legend and lore. I have given the standard Welsh spellings—which are often different from the spellings commonly used in English translations—and also, in the case of the *Mabinogion*, spellings from the original texts in Middle Welsh; in these latter cases, K has been read as the Coelbren letter Ci and V as the Coelbren letter Fi.

Entries marked (1 Mab.), (2 Mab.), and so on are proper names from the First, Second, etc. Branch of the *Mabinogion*. Entries marked *Barddas* are proper names from *Barddas*.

11	Iau	name of God
	OIO	var. of OIW
12	OIW	(concealed name of God)
	bo	var. of byw
14	OIU	var. of OIW
19	byw	life
21	Ced	earth goddess

22	Duw	God
47	Hu	(*Barddas*)
63	Beli	(2 Mab., *Barddas*)
78	Awen	spirit of inspiration
84	Don	(4 Mab.)
91	Gwawl	(1 Mab.)
93	Blodeued	var. of Blodeuwed
98	Blodeuwed	(4 Mab.)
100	Wledig	emperor
102	caer	castle
105	cawr	giant
111	Abred	(*Barddas*)
112	hen	old
	Iesu	Jesus
114	Goewin	(4 Mab.)
120	Einiged	var. of Einigan
122	Elen	(legendary figure)
125	Cradawc	(2 Mab.)
	mawr	great
127	Alawn	(*Barddas*)
128	Gwydion	(4 Mab.)
131	Gwydyon	var. of Gwydion
137	Dylan	(4 Mab.)
	Menw	(*Barddas*)
139	Ardudwy	(Mab. place name)
153	Menwyd	(*Barddas*)
158	sul	var. of sulw
163	sulw	sun
167	Arawn	(1 Mab.)
169	Bran	(2 Mab.)
171	Heilyn	(2 Mab.)
179	Einigan	(*Barddas*)
181	cadarn	mighty
182	Cernyw	Cornwall
	Einigain	var. of Einigan
	ynys	island
184	Iwerdon	Ireland
191	Ceridwen	(legendary figure)
192	arglwyd	prince, chieftain

193	Coriniaid	Coranians
197	Gwern	(2 Mab.)
199	Gronw	(4 Mab.)
	Gwron	(*Barddas*)
200	Einiger	var. of Einigan
202	Einigair	var. of Einigan
205	Gronwy	var. of Gronw
208	Deffrobani	the Summer Country
211	tad	father
216	Annwn	var. of Annwfn
224	Manawydan	var. of Manawyddan
233	Duw Tad	God the Father
235	coelbren	omen stick
236	Mynweir	(3 Mab.)
240	Mynord	(3 Mab.)
242	Macsen	(legendary figure)
246	Branwen	(2 Mab.)
	Einiged Gawr	var. of Einigan Gawr
249	Hu Gadarn	Hu the Mighty
254	Prydain	Britain
266	Aranrod	var. of Arianrhod
269	Arianrhod	(4 Mab.)
270	Pair Dadeni	Cauldron of Rebirth (2 Mab.)
271	Peir Dadeni	var. of Pair Dadeni
276	Abcedilros	the original Coelbren alphabet
281	Pryderi	(1–4 Mab.)
	Peredur	Percival, the knight of the Grail
283	brenhin	king
290	Tydain	(*Barddas*)
293	Gwydion ap Don	Gwydion son of Don
301	Math	(4 Mab.)
303	Aedd	(*Barddas*)
305	Einigan Gawr	(*Barddas*)
307	Dathyl	part of place name Caer Dathyl
308	Rhiannon	(1–3 Mab.)
309	Einigain Gawr	var. of Einigan Gawr
310	Einiget	var. of Einigan
319	Ceugant	(*Barddas*)
322	Eurosswyd	(2 Mab.)

324	Pendaran	(1 Mab.)
326	Einiger Gawr	var. of Einigan Gawr
328	Einigair Gawr	var. of Einigan Gawr
329	Dylan Eil Ton	(4 Mab.)
330	Penardun	(2 Mab.)
342	Macsen Wledig	Macsen the Emperor
351	Nissyen	(2 Mab.)
368	Caer Aranrod	var. of Caer Arianrhod
371	Caer Arianrhod	(4 Mab. place name)
383	Blodeuedd	(4 Mab.)
384	Ynys y Kedeirn	The Island of the Mighty
385	Ynys y Kedyrn	var. of Ynys y Kedeirn
	Gronw Pebyr	(4 Mab.)
386	Mathonwy	(4 Mab.)
409	Lleu	(4 Mab.)
	Caer Dathyl	(4 Mab. place name)
415	gwyddon	loremaster
421	Llwyd	(3 Mab.)
428	Arthur	Arthur
429	Taliesin	(legendary figure)
431	Arberth	(1 Mab. place name)
436	Einiget Gawr	var. of Einigan Gawr
439	Teirnon	var. of Teyrnon
442	Teyrnon	(1 Mab.)
451	Ynys Prydain	the island of Britain
456	Aranrot	var. of Arianrhod
491	Pwyll	(1 Mab.)
496	Llyr	(2 Mab.)
506	llys	royal court
511	Llwyt	var. of Llwyd
514	Manawyddan	(2–3 Mab.)
522	Kicfa	var. of Cigfa
523	Grist	Christ
526	gorsedd	bardic assembly
528	Dyfed	(Mab. place name)
531	Myrddin	Merlin
543	Cigfa	(3 Mab.)
558	Caer Aranrot	var. of Caer Arianrhod
562	Llundein	London

578	Plennydd	(*Barddas*)
579	Tydain Tad Awen	(*Barddas*)
592	Caswallawn	(2 Mab.)
628	Penllyn	(4 Mab. place name)
633	Teirgwaedd	(*Barddas*)
635	Iesu Grist	Jesus Christ
639	coelfain	omen stone
642	Hafgan	(1 Mab.)
664	moch	swine
716	Annwfn	(1 Mab. place name)
718	Dyfet	var. of Dyfed
722	Annwvyn	var.of Annwfn
732	gogyrfen	letter
740	gogyrfenau	letters
771	Mordwyd Tyllyon	(2 Mab.)
783	Harlech	(Mab. place name)
793	Hardlech	old spelling of Harlech
798	Bendigeidvran	Bran the Blessed (2 Mab.)
802	Addaf	Adam, the first man
835	Gilfathwy	var. Gilfaethwy
837	Gilfaethwy	(4 Mab.)
849	Hyfaidd	(1 Mab.)
852	Pendaran Dyved	(1 Mab.)
853	Efnissyen	(2 Mab.)
917	Gwynfydd	(*Barddas*)
957	Gorsedd Arberth	(1 & 3 Mab. place name)
960	Matholwch	(2 Mab.)
961	Hyfaidd Hen	(1 Mab.)
971	Llew Llaw Gyffes	(4 Mab.)
988	Bendigeitvran	var. of Bendigeidfran
1004	Mochnant	(4 Mab. place name)
1042	Pendaran Dyvet	old spelling of Pendaran Dyfed
1170	Dinas Dinllef	(4 Mab. place name)
1207	Llech Gronwy	(4 Mab. place name)
1266	Mochdref	(4 Mab. place name)
1456	Mochtref	var. of Mochdref

BIBLIOGRAPHY

Bardic sources

Williams, Edward (Iolo Morganwg), *Poems Lyric and Pastoral* (London: J. Nichols, 1794).

Williams, Taliesin, ed., *The Iolo Manuscripts* (London: Longman & Co., 1848).

Williams, Taliesin, ed., *Traethawd ar Hinafiaeth ac Awdurdodaeth Coelbren y Beirdd* (*Treatise on the Antiquity and Origin of the Coelbren of the Bards*), (Llandovery, Wales: William Rees, 1840).

Williams ab Ithel, John, ed. and trans., *Dosparth Edeyrn Davod Aur, or, The Ancient Welsh Grammar* (London: Longman & Co., 1856).

Williams ab Ithel, John, ed. and trans., *The Barddas of Iolo Morganwg* (reprinted York Beach, ME: Weiser Books, 2004; originally published 1862).

Other sources

Baker, Jim, *The Cunning Man's Handbook: The Practice of English Folk Magic 1550–1900* (London: Avalonia, 2013).

Bardon, Franz, *The Key to the True Quabbalah* (Wuppertal, Germany: Dieter Rüggeberg, 1971).

Barfield, Owen, *Saving the Appearances: A Study in Idolatry* (New York: Harcourt Brace Jovanovich, 1965).

Blum, Ralph, *The Book of Runes* (New York: St. Martin's Press, 1982).

Bonwick, James, *Irish Druids and Old Irish Religions* (New York: Dorset Press, 1983).

Charnell-White, Cathryn A., *Bardic Circles: National, Regional and Personal Identity in the Bardic Vision of Iolo Morganwg* (Cardiff: University of Wales Press, 2007).

Constantine, Mary Ann, *The Truth Against the World: Iolo Morganwg and Romantic Forgery* (Cardiff: University of Wales Press, 2007).

de Mille, Richard W., *The Don Juan Papers: Further Castaneda Controversies* (Santa Barbara, CA: Ross-Erikson Publishers, 1980).

Fortune, Dion, *Mystical Meditations on the Collects* (Wellingborough, UK: Aquarian, 1989).

Gerald of Wales, *The Journey Through Wales/The Description of Wales* (London: Penguin, 1978).

Greer, John Michael, *The Celtic Golden Dawn* (Woodbury, MN: Llewellyn Publications, 2013).

Greer, John Michael, The Coelbren of the Bards: A Practical Introduction, *Trilithon* 2 (2015), pp. 40–53.

Greer, John Michael, *The Druidry Handbook* (York Beach, ME: Weiser Books, 2006).

Greer, John Michael, The Myth of Einigan, *Trilithon* 1 (2014), pp. 19–26.

Hyginus, *The Myths of Hyginus*, trans. and ed. Mary Grant (Lawrence, KS: University of Kansas Press, 1960).

Jenkins, Geraint H. ed. *A Rattleskull Genius: The Many Faces of Iolo Morganwg* (Cardiff: University of Wales Press, 2005).

Jung, Carl, *Synchronicity: An Acausal Connecting Principle* (Princeton, NJ: Princeton University Press, 1960).

Lomer, Georg. *Seven Hermetic Letters*, trans. Gerhard Hanswille and Franca Gallo (Salt Lake City, UT: Merkur Publishing, 1997).

Mallet, Paul Henri, *Northern Antiquities*, trans. Thomas Percy (London: T. Carnan and Co., 1770).

Morris Jones, J., *A Welsh Grammar, Historical and Comparative* (Oxford: Clarendon Press, 1913).

Morrow, Avery, *The Sacred Science of Ancient Japan* (Rutland, VT: Bear & Company, 2014).

Murray, Liz and Colin, *The Celtic Tree Oracle* (New York: St. Martin's Press, 1988).

National Museum of Wales. Coelbren y Beirdd—The Bardic Alphabet. http://museumwales.ac.uk/en/888/; accessed 22 December 2014.

O'Flaherty, Roderick, *Ogygia, seu Rerum Hibernicarum Chronologia* (London: B. Tooke, 1685).

Pennick, Nigel, *Ogham and Coelbren: Keys to the Celtic Mysteries* (Chieveley, UK: Capall Ban, 2000).

Pennick, Nigel, *Games of the Gods* (York Beach, ME: Samuel Weiser, 1989).

Plato, *Cratylus*, trans. Benjamin Jowett, in *The Collected Dialogues of Plato*, ed. Edith Hamilton and Huntingdon Cairns (Princeton, NJ: Princeton University Press, 1961).

INDEX

Λ𝘝<𝘑>Ι𝘒ᴦΟᒉ

Printed in the USA
CPSIA information can be obtained
at www.ICGtesting.com
JSHW011417240823
47159JS00002B/33

9 781801 520621